BETA SIGMA PHI INTERNATIONAL

All-Occasion Casseroles Cookbook with Menus

© Favorite Recipes Press, A Division of Great American Opportunities Inc. MCMLXXXIII
P. O. Box 77, Nashville, Tennessee 37202
Library of Congress Cataloging in Publication Data on Page 127.

Dear Friends

Beta Sigma Phi is always proud to present a new cookbook and their latest *All-Occasion Casseroles Cookbook with Menus* is a double delight!

Not only does it feature casseroles, one of the most popular cookery methods of all time, but there's also a selection of menus for those times when nothing but a casserole will do. *Daddy Cooks Dinner* — and Mom has the night off — features an outdoor casserole and much more. Hearty fare that everyone loves is the key to *First Snow of the Season,* and it's not a lot of trouble for the cook. *The Hookup Was Hung Up* is the perfect menu for one of those days that starts out fine but falls apart by 5:00 p.m. And for a meal when you want to spend time with the guests and not in the kitchen . . . you'll love the ease and elegance of the *After Church Brunch* or *After The Concert* menus.

Ease, elegance and convenience — those are the hallmarks of casserole cookery. Magic for your menus! And if you're a busy homemaker who wants the best for your family, then you'll surely depend on *All-Occasion Casseroles Cookbook with Menus* . . . the latest presentation from Beta Sigma Phi!

Sincerely,

Marge Thomas

Marge Thomas
International Cookbook
Chairman
Beta Sigma Phi

Contents

Casseroles...

MEAN MENU MAGIC!!!

Today's casserole cookery ... it's versatile, convenient, economical *and* imaginative. Yet, who would guess anything so popular began under such lowly circumstances. No doubt, the earliest hunters often combined the day's game with wild roots and berries in a bubbling pot — especially when meat was scarce. American pioneers often used the "one-pot" method of cooking while on the trail because it was convenient, tasty and stretched the food supply.

The term "casserole" derives from the French word "casse" — a large utensil used by provencial French cooks who faithfully kept a "pot au feu" bubbling at the back of the hearth or stove. Whether the food supply was plentiful or not, there was always a nutritious meal ready to serve to a hungry family as well as to unexpected guests or travelers.

The one-pot cookery has been practical as long as there have been busy cooks, even in the crudest of kitchens. But the art of today's casserole cookery goes far beyond practical and nutritious. Today the casserole is also as adventurous as the cook pleases, featuring a range of favorite ingredients from apricots to zucchini.

Feel confident in building any menu around a casserole or several casseroles to be served buffet style. Whether it is to be the entree, a side dish, the dessert or all three, a casserole is menu magic!

CHOOSING THE RIGHT CONTAINER

The word *casserole* refers both to the food itself and to the dish in which the recipe is cooked and served. Choosing the right casserole dish should be simple, even though there are numerous shapes, sizes, colors and materials available to choose from. Most casseroles go from freezer to oven to table with complete ease, and are dishwasher safe — which all adds up to convenience for casserole cookery. There are some casseroles which require special care — such as those that need to be hand washed or soaked in hot water prior to being placed in a hot oven. But they are worth the trouble if they add beauty and pleasure to your dining enjoyment.

If you depend on casserole recipes in everyday menu planning and for special occasion menus, you should have several suitable dishes on hand. These include practical dishes, pretty dishes and extra casseroles for the freezer. The shallow, rectangular dishes in 1-, 1½, and 2-quart sizes are the basics in any collection. Individual sizes (1-1½ cup size) are also very useful — especially for freezer and microwave use. Many of the better china and tableware manufacturers include an array of casseroles in the selection of accessory pieces to favorite patterns. Whether you choose matching dishes or glazed pottery, stainless steel, heatproof glass, earthenware or enamelware, be sure your choice of casserole dishes suits your needs. Easy care non-stick linings, freezer and ovenproof, pretty and durable — these are the qualities that make casserole dishes and casserole cookery magic for meal planning!

YOUR CASSEROLE RECIPE

Here is where the cook's imagination can really soar! Most recipes have a featured ingredient — whether it be a meat, vegetable, fruit, pasta, cheese or any combination of favorite foods. Beyond the feature flavor, there are no hard and fast rules for casserole cookery. Casseroles are adaptable!

— Casseroles featuring beef, pork, veal, lamb, or game are a delightfully different way to serve your favorite meat — and in a variety of ways! Leftover portions of meats are ideal for casserole cookery, as they can be very elegant and still make the most of your food budget.

— Ground beef and casserole cookery seem to have been made for each other! Ground beef is very economical and can be prepared in a variety of flavors, from mild to zesty, from Oriental to Italian, from casual to elegant — so that your family never grows tired of ground beef in the menu.

— Fish and seafood, when bought in season, can be more economical than meat. Make use of these in casserole cookery, and your menus will compare with those of many of the best restaurants in the world. Unless you live near the coast where seafood is common at mealtimes, seafood casseroles will be a welcome change of pace.

— For flavor variety and economy, poultry is comparable only to ground beef in casserole cookery. Purchase plenty of poultry when it is on "special." Then boil it, remove the meat from the bones, and freeze the meat for convenient and ready use in casseroles.

— Side dish casseroles featuring vegetables, eggs, cheese, pasta, rice or other cereals (and combinations of these) offer a wide variety of ways to add interest to mealtime. They are also delicious entrees for "meatless" meals, especially when they include eggs and/or cheese.

— If no meal is complete for your family without a dessert, casserole cookery makes it easy! Often, dessert casseroles can be prepared in advance so that the cook is free to enjoy the meal with her family and friends. Dessert casseroles are also an excellent way to serve eggs, dairy products and fruit in the diet.

— Take care with the topping for your casserole: choose it for flavor and color, but most of all to make your casserole as attractive as it is tasty. Raw vegetable garnishes add color and shape. Herbed bread crumbs add taste variety. For seafood casseroles, try artfully shaped lemon twists, slices or wedges. Consider colorful and delicious combinations of cheese triangles, olive slices, parsley, etc. The possibilities are as exciting as they are limitless!

Once you become familiar with a casserole recipe, feel free to experiment. If the suggested seasonings are not quite what you want, make the change that best suits you. Or if a recipe calls for a certain amount of condensed mushroom soup and you prefer to use condensed celery soup, do it! If you prefer to use 1 pound of ground beef with 1 pound of ground pork when a recipe calls for 2 pounds of ground beef, make the switch! Or if a recipe calls for 2 cups of diced chicken and you're a little short, continue with confidence. Depending on the leftover meats and vegetables in your refrigerator or freezer, you can scramble ingredients to your heart's content. Casserole cookery is economical and nutritious, but it should be fun and rewarding as well. There's nothing like a casserole for creative magic for your meal planning!

FREEZING FAVORITE CASSEROLES

For real menu magic in casserole cookery, take advantage of the convenience of freezing favorite casserole recipes. Whenever you prepare a recipe, double it so that you can serve one and freeze the other for an "instant" meal later. Follow the basic rules for freezing food when freezing casseroles: use moisture and vapor proof freezer paper and freezer tape to wrap the packages; label and date all packages so that none will remain in the freezer for too long. If you have enough freezer-to-oven casserole dishes, freeze the extra casserole in the dish it will be heated in later. If you can't spare a dish for the freezer, here is a handy trick: line the baking dish with foil, leaving plenty on the edges. Fill dish with the casserole mixture; freeze solid. Remove the foil-lined frozen block of food from the dish, seal foil tightly around food, and return to the freezer. Unwrap frozen casserole and place in original container to cook and serve.

Most casserole mixtures should be partially cooked before freezing, then thoroughly reheated after thawing. You can also reheat the frozen mixture in the oven at the cooking temperature suggested in the recipe. Allow a longer baking time when taking a casserole directly from the freezer to the oven. If possible, stir the mixture several times during the thawing/baking process to avoid singed edges or a frozen center. Add any desired topping during the last 15 to 30 minutes of heating time.

Follow these tips when freezing casseroles:

- Undercook casseroles that are to be frozen so that they will not overcook when reheated.
- Fried foods, salad greens and raw vegetables do not freeze well; they lose their crispness.
- Diced potatoes should be added just before baking; they become mushy and fall apart if frozen.
- Fats become rancid after 2 months in the freezer; use these sparingly in casseroles to be frozen.
- Most seasonings, as well as garlic, cloves, pimento and green pepper become stronger when frozen, so use these sparingly. Onions tend to lose their flavor.

Although casserole-style cookery goes back to the earliest kitchens, it is perfectly suited to modern microwave cooking. This convenience is multiplied when you use both your freezer and your microwave oven for your casseroles. For best results, follow carefully the preparation, cooking and thawing suggestions found in the handbook or cookbook that came with your microwave oven.

When it comes to the magic of casserole cookery, Beta Sigma Phis know all the tricks! And with this collection of casserole recipes and menus, they want to share the magic with you. If you're not yet a casserole cook, this great new cookbook will show you how. Whether you've been cooking for years or are just beginning, you'll find this collection as timeless as it is versatile and practical. There's no question about it — *CASSEROLES ARE MENU MAGIC!*

> **Crab Meat Dip Deluxe**
> *BSP Desserts & Party Foods, p. 62*
> **Hawaiian Barbecued Chicken**
> **Quadicttine Spinach**
> **Carrot-Rice Casserole**
> **Scalloped Corn-Mac**
> **Oven-Fried Potatoes**
> **Green Beans Goldenrod**
> **Banana-Walnut Bread**
> *BSP All-Occasion Casseroles, p. 104*
> **Scalloped Pineapple**
> **Wheaties and Coconut Cookies**
> *BSP Desserts & Party Foods, p. 98*
> **Tangy Punch**
> *BSP Desserts & Party Foods, p. 54*

Daddy Cooks Dinner

HAWAIIAN BARBECUED CHICKEN

1 broiler-fryer, quartered
1/4 c. melted butter
1/2 tsp. salt
2 c. canned applesauce
1/2 c. apple juice
2 tbsp. lemon juice
1 tsp. grated lemon rind
1/2 c. packed brown sugar
1/2 tsp. dry mustard
1/2 c. toasted slivered almonds

Brush ..... chicken with butter and season with salt.
Brown ..... on both sides over hot coals.
Place ...... chicken on heavy foil shaped into 2-inch deep pan.
Place ...... pan on grill.
Combine ... remaining ingredients in bowl, mixing well.
Spoon ..... applesauce mixture over chicken.
Cook ...... loosely covered, for 45 minutes, turning and basting once.

Cook ...... uncovered, for 15 minutes longer.
Yields ..... 4 servings.

Photograph for this recipe above.

QUADICTTINE SPINACH

1/3 c. minced onion
2 cloves of garlic, crushed
1/2 c. diced carrots
3 celery stalks, diced
1/2 c. olive oil
1 lb. ground beef
2 1/2 c. tomatoes
2/3 c. tomato paste
1 tsp. salt
1/2 tsp. pepper
1/4 lb. thin noodles, cooked
1 pkg. frozen chopped spinach, cooked
1/2 c. buttered fresh bread crumbs
1/2 c. grated American cheese
Parmesan cheese

Saute ..... onion, garlic, carrots and celery in olive oil in Dutch oven until light brown.

Add ...... ground beef.

Cook ...... until light brown, stirring until crumbly.

Add ...... tomatoes, tomato paste, salt and pepper.

Simmer .... for 2 to 2 1/2 hours.

Chill ...... for several hours.

Stir .... in noodles and spinach.

Top .... with bread crumbs and cheeses.

Bake ...... in moderate oven until brown and bubbly.

Yields ..... 8 servings.

Delores Ann Stouffer
Laureate Beta, Smithsburg, Maryland

CARROT-RICE CASSEROLE

3 c. shredded carrots
2/3 c. rice
1/4 tsp. salt
2 c. shredded Cheddar cheese
1 can cream of celery soup
1 tsp. minced onion

Simmer .... carrots with rice and salt in 1 1/2 cups water in saucepan for 25 minutes.

Stir .... in 1 1/2 cups cheese, soup, onion and 1/2 cup water.

Spoon ..... into 1 1/2-quart casserole.

Bake ...... at 350 degrees for 1 hour.

Top .... with remaining 1/2 cup cheese.

Bake ...... for 2 minutes longer or until cheese melts.

Yields ..... 6-8 servings.

Jary Nan Nelson
Epsilon Nu, Stayton, Oregon

SCALLOPED CORN-MAC

1 1-lb. can cream-style corn
1 1-lb. can whole kernel corn
1 c. macaroni
1/2 c. melted margarine
1 c. cubed Velveeta cheese

Combine ... all ingredients in bowl, mixing well.

Spoon ..... into 2-quart casserole.

Bake ...... at 350 degrees for 1 hour.

Yields ..... 8 servings.

Mrs. Burdette L. Konzak
Xi Gamma Zeta, Harvard, Nebraska

OVEN-FRIED POTATOES

3 med. potatoes, cut into 1/8-in. wedges
1/4 c. oil

1 tbsp. Parmesan cheese
1/2 tsp. salt
1/4 tsp. garlic powder
1/4 tsp. each paprika, pepper

Place ...... potatoes in single layer in 9 x 13-inch baking pan.

Combine ... remaining ingredients in bowl, mixing well.

Brush ..... over potatoes.

Bake ...... at 375 degrees for 45 minutes, basting occasionally with oil mixture.

Yields ..... 4-6 servings.

Jean R. Furr
Xi Phi, Concord, North Carolina

GREEN BEANS GOLDENROD

1 tbsp. butter, melted
1 tbsp. flour
1/4 tsp. salt
Dash of pepper
1/2 c. milk
2 hard-boiled eggs, separated
1/2 c. mayonnaise
1 can green beans
Paprika

Blend ..... first 4 ingredients in saucepan.

Stir .... in milk gradually.

Cook ...... until thick, stirring constantly; remove from heat.

Add ...... chopped egg white and mayonnaise.

Cook ...... green beans in saucepan until heated through; drain.

Place ...... green beans in serving dish.

Top .... with sauce.

Sprinkle ... with sieved egg yolk and paprika.

Sharon S. Williams
Xi Gamma Iota, Hixson, Tennessee

SCALLOPED PINEAPPLE

1 stick margarine, melted
2 c. sugar
1 lg. can crushed pineapple
2 c. bread crumbs
2 eggs
1/2 tsp. vanilla extract
1/2 c. milk

Mix .... ingredients in order given in 2-quart casserole.

Bake ...... at 350 degrees for 1 hour or until brown.

Yields ..... 8 servings.

Betty A. Schmaltz
Xi Sigma, Knoxville, Tennessee

Pecan-Beef Dip
BSP Desserts & Party Foods, p. 63
Rock Lobster Divan
Broccoli-Onion Deluxe
Sweet Potato and Apple Casserole
Spinach Casserole
Nosotros Vegetable Casserole
Green Bean Caesar
Peach Bread
BSP All-Occasion Casseroles, p. 105
Golden Champagne
BSP Desserts & Party Foods, p. 52
Swedish Osta Kaka
Angostura Chocolate Dessert
BSP Desserts & Party Foods, p. 106

Neighborhood Gourmet Club Dinner

ROCK LOBSTER DIVAN

3 8-oz. packages South African rock
   lobster tails
Salt
1/4 c. butter, melted
1/4 c. flour
1 c. light cream
1 c. white wine
2 tbsp. chopped chives
1 c. grated Cheddar cheese
Pepper to taste
2 10-oz. packages frozen asparagus spears,
   cooked, drained

Place ...... rock lobster tails in boiling salted water.
Bring ...... to a boil.
Boil .... for 2 minutes; drain and drench with cold water.
Remove ... lobster meat in one piece.
Blend ..... butter and flour in saucepan.
Stir .... in cream and wine gradually.
Cook ...... over low heat until thick, stirring constantly.
Stir .... in chives, cheese and seasonings to taste.
Arrange .... asparagus spears in 6 shallow baking dishes.
Top .... with lobster tails.
Spoon ..... cheese sauce over asparagus and lobster.
Broil ...... until golden brown.
Yields ..... 6 servings.

Photograph for this recipe above.

BROCCOLI-ONION DELUXE

1/4 c. butter, melted
2 tbsp. flour
1/4 tsp. salt
Dash of pepper
1 c. milk
1 3-oz. package cream cheese, softened
1 lb. broccoli, cooked, chopped
2 c. frozen small onions
1/2 c. shredded sharp American cheese
1 c. soft bread crumbs

Blend ..... 2 tablespoons butter and next 4 ingredients in saucepan.
Simmer .... until thickened, stirring constantly.
Stir .... in cream cheese.
Combine ... with vegetables in casserole, mixing lightly.
Top .... with American cheese.
Combine ... remaining 2 tablespoons butter with bread crumbs.

Sprinkle ... over casserole.
Bake ...... at 350 degrees for 40 minutes or until bubbly.
Yields ..... 6 servings.

Kathy Samol
Mu Mu, Edinboro, Pennsylvania

SWEET POTATO AND APPLE CASSEROLE

5 c. sliced cooked sweet potatoes
3 c. sliced apples
1/2 c. packed brown sugar
2 tbsp. orange juice
1/2 tsp. salt
2 tbsp. margarine

Layer ..... sweet potatoes and apples in greased casserole.
Sprinkle ... with brown sugar.
Combine ... juice and salt with 1/2 cup water.
Pour ...... over layers.
Dot .... with margarine.
Bake ...... at 350 degrees for 35 to 40 minutes or until apples are tender.

Mary Ann Mietty
Beta Sigma Phi No. 4388, Painesville, Ohio

SPINACH CASSEROLE

3 10-oz. packages chopped spinach,
thawed, well drained
1 pt. sour cream
1 pkg. onion soup mix

Combine ... all ingredients in bowl, mixing well.
Spoon ..... into casserole.
Bake ...... at 350 degrees for 30 minutes.
Yields ..... 6 servings.

Carrie A. Bogle
Laureate Zeta, Reno, Nevada

NOSOTROS VEGETABLE CASSEROLE

1 20-oz. can French-style green beans
1 c. mushroom soup
1 5-oz. can water chestnuts, drained
1 5-oz. can bamboo shoots, drained
1/2 can sliced blanched almonds
Salt and pepper to taste
1 3 1/2-oz. can French-fried onion rings

Drain ..... beans, reserving 1/4 cup liquid.
Heat ...... soup and reserved liquid in saucepan.
Stir .... in green beans and remaining ingredients except onions.

Spoon ..... into greased casserole.
Bake ...... in moderate oven for 25 minutes.
Top .... with onions.
Bake ...... for 5 minutes longer.
Yields ..... 8-10 servings.

Norma Truitt
Xi Psi Beta, Beeville, Texas

GREEN BEAN CAESAR

1 lb. fresh green beans
2 tbsp. oil
1 tbsp. cider vinegar
1 or 2 cloves of garlic, minced
Salt to taste
Pepper and oregano to taste
2 tbsp. melted butter
1/4 c. bread crumbs
1 to 2 tbsp. Parmesan cheese

Cook ...... beans in water in saucepan for 20 minutes; drain.
Combine ... oil, vinegar, garlic, salt, pepper and oregano in bowl, mixing well.
Add ...... green beans, mixing well.
Spoon ..... into 1 1/2-quart casserole.
Combine ... butter and crumbs in bowl, mixing well.
Sprinkle ... crumbs and cheese over casserole.
Bake ...... at 350 degrees for 15 to 20 minutes.
Yields ..... 4-6 servings.

Rhonda Thompson
Exemplar Xi Epsilon Zeta, Fairfield, Ohio

SWEDISH OSTA KAKA

4 eggs, well beaten
3 c. cottage cheese
1 c. sugar
3/4 c. flour
2 c. half and half
1/2 tsp. vanilla extract

Mix .... first 3 ingredients in large bowl.
Combine ... flour and half and half in small bowl, stirring to make smooth paste.
Add ...... to cottage cheese mixture, mixing well.
Stir .... in vanilla.
Pour ...... into lightly greased 1 1/2-quart casserole.
Place ...... in pan of water.
Bake ...... at 400 degrees for 1 hour or until top is brown.
Spoon ..... into bowls.
Serve ...... with lingonberries or other sweetened berries and whipped topping.
Yields ..... 4-6 servings.

Jacque Dale
Beta Tau, Summerville, South Carolina

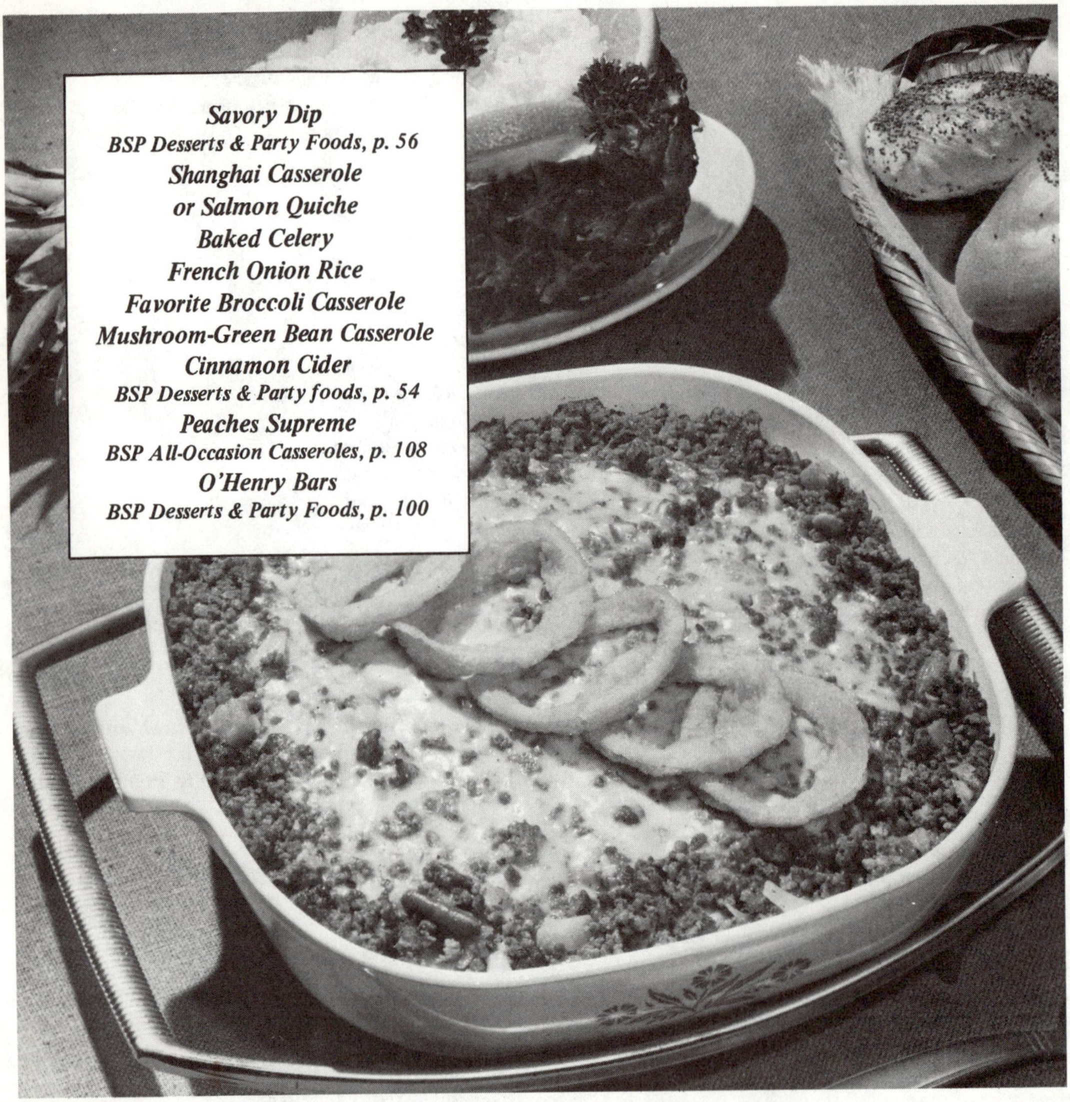

Savory Dip
BSP Desserts & Party Foods, p. 56
Shanghai Casserole
or Salmon Quiche
Baked Celery
French Onion Rice
Favorite Broccoli Casserole
Mushroom-Green Bean Casserole
Cinnamon Cider
BSP Desserts & Party foods, p. 54
Peaches Supreme
BSP All-Occasion Casseroles, p. 108
O'Henry Bars
BSP Desserts & Party Foods, p. 100

The Hookup Was Hung Up

SHANGHAI CASSEROLE

2 lb. ground beef
1 c. finely chopped onion
1 10-oz. package frozen mixed vegetables
1 can mushroom soup
1 tsp. salt
1/4 tsp. pepper
1 tbsp. soy sauce
2 c. chopped celery
1 3-oz. can Chinese noodles

Brown . . . . . ground beef with onion in skillet, stirring until crumbly; drain.
Cook . . . . . . mixed vegetables according to package directions for 5 minutes; drain.
Add . . . . . . vegetables, 1/2 cup water and remaining ingredients except noodles to ground beef mixture, mixing well.
Spoon . . . . . into 2 1/2-quart casserole.
Bake . . . . . . covered, at 350 degrees for 25 minutes.
Sprinkle . . . with noodles.
Bake . . . . . . uncovered, for 5 minutes longer.
Yields . . . . . 6-8 servings.

Photograph for this recipe above.

SALMON QUICHE

1/2 onion, chopped
Butter
2 sm. cans evaporated milk
4 eggs, beaten
1 lg. can salmon
2 c. grated cheese
Salt and pepper to taste
1 unbaked pie shell

Saute ..... onion in butter in skillet.
Add ...... evaporated milk, eggs, salmon, cheese, salt and pepper, mixing well.
Pour ...... into pie shell.
Bake ...... at 375 degrees for 30 to 40 minutes.

June Willey
Preceptor Zeta Phi, Sunnyvale, California

BAKED CELERY

4 c. chopped celery
1 5-oz. can water chestnuts
1 can cream of chicken soup
2 tbsp. diced pimentos
1/2 c. bread crumbs
1/4 c. slivered almonds
2 tbsp. melted margarine

Cook ...... celery in a small amount of water in saucepan for 10 minutes; drain.
Combine ... with water chestnuts, soup and pimentos.
Mix .... crumbs, almonds and margarine in bowl.
Stir .... half the crumb mixture into soup mixture.
Spoon ..... into 1 1/2-quart casserole.
Top .... with remaining crumb mixture.
Bake ...... at 350 degrees for 30 to 35 minutes.
Yields ..... 6-8 servings.

Velda M. Kloke
Xi Gamma Zeta, Harvard, Nebraska

FRENCH ONION RICE

1 1/2 c. rice
1 can French onion soup
1 can beef broth
1 stick butter
1/2 c. sliced water chestnuts

Combine ... all ingredients in 1 1/2-quart casserole.
Bake ...... at 350 degrees for 50 minutes.

Donna Thomas
Alpha Beta, McComb, Mississippi

FAVORITE BROCCOLI CASSEROLE

1 10-oz. package chopped broccoli
1 8-oz. jar Cheez Whiz
1 can cream of mushroom soup
1 c. cooked rice
1/2 c. chopped onion
4 tbsp. butter

Combine ... all ingredients in 2-quart buttered casserole.
Bake ...... at 350 degrees for 25 to 30 minutes.
Yields ..... 6 servings.

Eleonora Free
Preceptor Beta Chi, Oswego, Kansas

MUSHROOM-GREEN BEAN CASSEROLE

1 lb. ground beef
1 can cream of mushroom soup
1 4-oz. can mushrooms, drained
1 can green beans, drained
1 lb. Italian cheese, grated
Tater Tots

Brown ..... ground beef in skillet, stirring until crumbly; drain.
Add ...... soup, mushrooms, green beans and half the cheese, mixing well.
Spoon ..... into casserole.
Bake ...... in moderate oven until heated through.
Prepare .... Tater Tots using package directions.
Top .... casserole with remaining cheese.
Bake ...... for 10 minutes longer or until cheese melts.
Arrange .... Tater Tots over top.
Yields ..... 6 servings.

Janet Buchholz
Xi Beta Psi, Duttmer, Missouri

Tasty Cheese Puffs
BSP Desserts & Party Foods, p. 70
Ham and Cheese Strata
Stuffed French Toast
Apricot Fruit Salad
Vegetables a la Eleanor
Hash Brown Casserole
Pam's Cheddar Squash Bake
Pink Rhubarb Pie
Hot Buttered Rum
BSP Desserts & Party Foods, p. 54

After Church Brunch

HAM AND CHEESE STRATA

8 slices white bread
2 c. shredded Cheddar cheese
1 1/2 c. chopped baked ham
1 2-oz. can sliced mushrooms, drained
1/4 c. chopped parsley
2 1/4 c. milk
4 eggs, slightly beaten
1 tsp. salt
1/4 tsp. dry mustard
1/8 tsp. paprika
Dash of pepper

Trim . . . . . . crusts from 5 slices bread, reserving crusts; cut in half diagonally and set aside.
Place . . . . . . remaining 3 slices bread and crusts in buttered 9-inch baking dish.
Layer . . . . . cheese, ham, mushrooms and parsley over bread.
Arrange . . . . bread triangles in 2 rows over layers.
Combine . . . remaining ingredients in bowl, mixing well.
Pour . . . . . . over bread.
Chill . . . . . . covered, for 3 hours to overnight.
Bake . . . . . . at 325 degrees for 45 to 60 minutes or until knife inserted in center comes out clean.
Let . . . . stand for 5 minutes before serving.
Yields . . . . . 6 servings.

Photograph for this recipe on opposite page.

STUFFED FRENCH TOAST

1 8-oz. package cream cheese, softened
1 1/2 tsp. vanilla extract
1/2 c. chopped walnuts
1 16-oz. loaf French bread
4 eggs, beaten
1 c. whipping cream
1/2 tsp. nutmeg
1 12-oz. jar apricot preserves
1/2 c. orange juice

Beat . . . . . . cream cheese with 1 teaspoon vanilla in bowl until fluffy.
Stir . . . . in walnuts.
Cut . . . . bread into 1 1/2-inch slices with pocket in each.
Spoon . . . . . 1 1/2 tablespoons cream cheese mixture into each pocket.
Combine . . . eggs with cream, 1/2 teaspoon vanilla and nutmeg in bowl, mixing well.
Dip . . . . filled bread in egg mixture.
Brown . . . . . on both sides on lightly greased griddle.
Cook . . . . . . preserves and orange juice in saucepan until heated through.

Drizzle . . . . over hot French toast.
Yields . . . . . 10-12 servings.

Mary Bowman
Laureate Eta, Warner Robins, Georgia

APRICOT FRUIT SALAD

1 20-oz. can crushed pineapple
1 6-oz. package apricot gelatin
2 bananas, chopped
1 c. miniature marshmallows
1/4 c. flour
1 c. sugar
1/4 c. butter
2 eggs, lightly beaten
2 3-oz. packages cream cheese, softened
1 pkg. whipped topping mix

Drain . . . . . pineapple, reserving juice.
Dissolve . . . gelatin in 2 cups boiling water in bowl.
Stir . . . . in 2 cups cold water, bananas, marshmallows and pineapple.
Pour . . . . . . into 9 x 13-inch dish.
Chill . . . . . . until firm.
Add . . . . . . enough water to reserved juice to measure 1 cup.
Blend . . . . . with flour, sugar, butter and eggs in saucepan.
Cook . . . . . . over medium heat until thick, stirring constantly.
Add . . . . . . cream cheese, stirring until melted; cool.
Spoon . . . . . over gelatin.
Prepare . . . . whipped topping using package directions.
Spread . . . . over cream cheese layer.
Chill . . . . . . until serving time.
Cut . . . . into squares to serve.
Yields . . . . . 20 servings.

Karen McKenzie
Upsilon, Springdale, Arkansas

VEGETABLES A LA ELEANOR

1 pkg. frozen California vegetables
1 jar Cheez Whiz
1 stick butter, melted
Crushed butter crackers

Layer . . . . . vegetables and Cheez Whiz in casserole.
Mix . . . . butter with cracker crumbs.
Spread . . . . over casserole.
Bake . . . . . . at 350 degrees for 30 to 45 minutes or until brown and bubbly.
Yields . . . . . 6-8 servings.

Eleanor Grover
Laureate Iota, Lee's Summit, Missouri

HASHED BROWN CASSEROLE

1 lg. package frozen hashed brown potatoes
1 can cream of celery soup
1 can cream of mushroom soup
1/2 c. each chopped onions, green peppers
Paprika
Chopped parsley

Combine ... first 5 ingredients in bowl, mixing well.
Spoon ..... into greased 9 x 13-inch baking dish.
Top .... with paprika and parsley.
Bake ...... at 350 degrees for 1 1/2 hours.
Yields ..... 10 servings.

Viola Whitten
Xi Epsilon, Eakly, Oklahoma

PAM'S CHEDDAR SQUASH BAKE

2 lb. yellow squash, trimmed
2 eggs, separated
1 c. sour cream
2 tbsp. flour
1 1/2 c. shredded Cheddar cheese
5 slices crisp-cooked bacon, crumbled
1/3 c. fine dry bread crumbs
2 tbsp. melted butter

Cook ...... squash in boiling salted water to cover for 15 to 20 minutes or until tender; drain and slice.
Mix .... slightly beaten egg yolks with sour cream and flour in bowl.
Fold ...... in stiffly beaten egg whites.
Layer ..... squash, egg mixture, cheese and bacon in 7 x 12-inch baking dish.
Mix .... crumbs with butter.
Sprinkle ... around edge.
Garnish .... with a few squash slices and bacon.
Bake ...... at 350 degrees for 20 to 25 minutes or until bubbly.
Yields ..... 8-11 servings.

Pam Daugherty
Delta Kappa, Cape Coral, Florida

PINK RHUBARB PIE

1 egg, beaten
1 1/3 c. sugar
3 tbsp. cornstarch
1/4 tsp. red food coloring
1   8-oz. carton strawberry yogurt
2 c. chopped rhubarb
2 pkg. frozen strawberries
1 recipe 2-crust pie pastry

Combine ... first 4 ingredients in bowl, mixing well.
Fold ...... in yogurt, rhubarb and strawberries.
Spoon ..... into crust.
Top .... with remaining pastry, cutting vents and crimping edges.
Bake ...... at 375 degrees for 50 minutes or until golden.
Yields ..... 6 servings.

Barbara Wimer
Xi Iota, Lewiston, Idaho

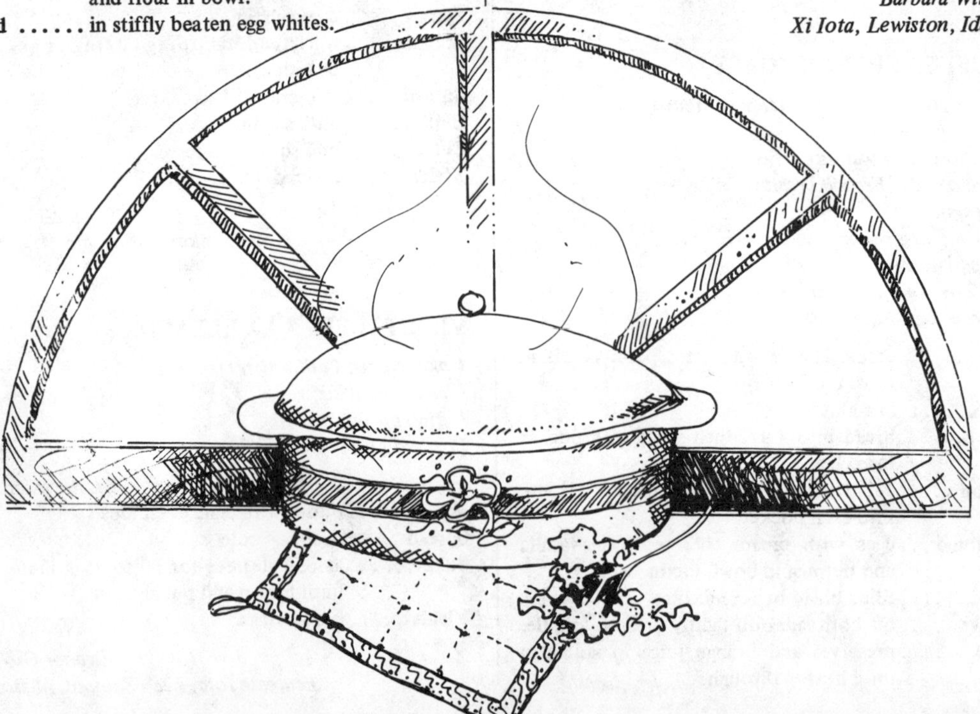

> *Savory Dip*
> *BSP Desserts & Party Foods, p. 56*
> *Aromatic Potato Casserole*
> *or Beef Burgundy*
> *Spinach Salad*
> *Asparagus Casserole*
> *Last Minute Rolls*
> *Instant Parfaits*
> *Caramel-Chocolate Squares*
> *BSP Desserts & Party Foods, p. 98*
> *Sheryl's Delight*

Last Minute Celebration

BEEF BURGUNDY

2 lb. stew meat
2 cans cream of mushroom soup
3 tbsp. Sherry
1 pkg. dry onion soup mix
1 c. sour cream
2 c. rice, cooked

Brown . . . . . stew meat in skillet.
Layer . . . . . with soup, Sherry, onion soup mix and sour cream in 9 x 13-inch casserole.
Bake . . . . . . at 250 degrees for 5 hours.
Serve . . . . . . with hot rice.
Yields . . . . . 6-8 servings.

Brenda Stolte
Alpha Psi Delta, Odessa, Texas

SPINACH SALAD

1 jar coleslaw dressing
1/2 jar chopped pickled beets, drained
1 tsp. Beau Monde seasoning
Beet juice
2 bunches fresh spinach, washed, torn
1 bunch green onions, chopped
3 or 4 hard-boiled eggs, sliced
1/2 lb. crisp-cooked bacon, crumbled

Combine . . . first 3 ingredients with enough beet juice to color dressing light pink.
Layer . . . . . remaining ingredients in salad bowl.
Pour . . . . . . dressing over salad just before serving.

Barbara Corn
Xi Alpha Chi, Glendale, Arizona

AROMATIC POTATO CASSEROLE

4 tbsp. butter, melted
4 tbsp. flour
2 c. milk
1 tsp. salt
Dash of pepper
1 tsp. angostura bitters
2 1-lb. cans potatoes, drained chopped
2 4-oz. cans Vienna sausage
1 3-oz. package cream cheese, cubed

Blend ..... butter and flour in saucepan.
Stir .... in milk gradually.
Cook ...... until thick, stirring constantly.
Season .... with salt, pepper and bitters.
Layer ..... potatoes and sausages in casserole.
Cover ..... with sauce.
Dot .... with cream cheese.
Bake ...... at 350 degrees until brown and bubbly.

Photograph for this recipe on page 19.

ASPARAGUS CASSEROLE

1/4 c. flour
1 tsp. salt
1/4 tsp. pepper
1/3 c. butter, melted
2 sm. cans asparagus tips
Milk
1 pimento, chopped
4 hard-boiled eggs, sliced
1/2 c. grated cheese
1/2 c. fine bread crumbs

Blend ..... flour, salt and pepper into half the butter in saucepan.
Drain ..... asparagus, reserving liquid.
Add ...... enough milk to reserved liquid to measure 2 cups.
Stir .... into flour mixture.
Cook ...... over low heat until thickened, stirring constantly; remove from heat.
Stir .... in pimento.
Reserve .... several asparagus tips for garnish.
Layer ..... half the asparagus, eggs, sauce and cheese in 1 1/2-quart casserole.
Repeat .... layers with remaining ingredients.
Top .... with bread crumbs and reserved asparagus.
Drizzle .... remaining butter over top.
Bake ...... at 425 degrees for 20 minutes.
Yields ..... 8-10 servings.

Marie Stephenson
Xi Gamma Iota, Chattanooga, Tennessee

LAST-MINUTE ROLLS

1 1/4 c. milk
2 1/2 tbsp. sugar
1 1/2 tsp. salt
1/4 c. shortening
2 pkg. yeast
3 1/2 c. flour

Scald ...... milk with sugar, salt and shortening in large saucepan; cool to lukewarm.
Dissolve ... yeast in 1/4 cup lukewarm water.
Stir .... into milk mixture.
Add ...... flour, mixing until just moistened.
Fill .... greased muffin cups half full.
Let .... rise for 35 minutes or until doubled in bulk.
Bake ...... at 425 degrees for 20 minutes.
Yields ..... 14 rolls.

Amber A. Horovenko
Preceptor Delta Beta, Long Beach, California

INSTANT PARFAITS

1 pkg. vanilla instant pudding mix
1 1/2 c. milk
1/2 c. heavy cream
1/2 tsp. angostura bitters
1 can cling peaches, drained
6 lg. macaroons, crumbled

Prepare .... pudding according to package directions, using 1 1/2 cups milk, 1/2 cup cream and adding bitters.
Spoon ..... pudding, peaches and crumbs alternately into parfait glasses until all ingredients are used, ending with pudding.
Chill ...... for 5 minutes or longer.

Photograph for this recipe on page 19.

SHERYL'S DELIGHT

2 cans fruit-flavored Hawaiian punch
2 12-oz. cans frozen lemonade
2 6-oz. cans frozen limeade
1 pt. (about) rum

Combine ... first 3 ingredients in punch bowl, mixing well.
Stir .... in rum.
Yields ..... 20-30 servings.

Jan Burnett
Beta Tau, Sedalia, Missouri

Tuna TV Dinner Italiano
or Cantonese Tuna Packets
Special Corn Casserole
Marinated Carrot Casserole
Saucy Sweet Potatoes
Casserole Onion Bread
Twice-Chocolate Ice Cream
BSP Desserts & Party Foods, p. 32
Chocolate Eclair
Nancy's Fruit Punch
BSP Desserts & Party Foods, p. 52

Kids Cook

TUNA TV DINNER ITALIANO

1 sm. eggplant, sliced 1/4-in. thick
2 cans oil-pack tuna
1/2 tsp. salt
1/4 tsp. basil
1/4 tsp. pepper
2 tsp. lemon juice
1 onion, sliced
1 1-lb. can tomatoes

Place . . . . . . eggplant on four 12-inch foil squares.
Combine . . . remaining ingredients in bowl, mixing well.
Spoon . . . . . over eggplant, folding to seal.
Bake . . . . . . at 400 degrees for 25 minutes or until eggplant is tender.
Garnish . . . . with Parmesan cheese.
Yields . . . . . 4 servings.

Photograph for this recipe above.

CANTONESE TUNA PACKETS

2 cans oil-pack tuna
1 bunch scallions, sliced
1 6-oz. can water chestnuts, drained, sliced
2 tbsp. each soy sauce, Sherry
1/8 tsp. each ginger, pepper
1 red pepper, cut in strips
1 6-oz. package Chinese pea pods, thawed

Combine . . . all ingredients in bowl, mixing well.
Spoon . . . . . onto four 12-inch foil squares, folding to seal.
Bake . . . . . . at 350 degrees for 20 to 30 minutes or until heated through.
Garnish . . . . with cashews.

Photograph for this recipe on page 21.

SPECIAL CORN CASSEROLE

1/2 c. margarine
1 17-oz. can whole kernel corn
1 17-oz. can cream-style corn
1 8 1/2- oz. package corn bread mix
2 eggs, beaten
1 c. sour cream
1 c. grated sharp Cheddar cheese

Melt . . . . . . margarine in 9 x 13-inch baking dish.
Fold . . . . . . in corn, corn bread mix and eggs gently with fork.
Spoon . . . . . sour cream over mixture and fold in.
Top . . . . with cheese.
Bake . . . . . . at 350 degrees for 20 to 30 minutes or until firm.
Cool . . . . . . slightly before cutting into squares.
Serve . . . . . . hot or at room temperature.

Hazel Milton
Laureate Iota, Independence, Missouri

MARINATED CARROT CASSEROLE

1 can tomato soup
1/2 c. vinegar
1 tsp. mustard
1 c. sugar
1 1/2 tsp. salt
5 c. sliced carrots, cooked, drained
1 med. onion, sliced into rings
1 green pepper, sliced into rings

Combine . . . first 5 ingredients in saucepan.
Cook . . . . . . until sugar is dissolved.
Pour . . . . . . over remaining ingredients in bowl.
Chill . . . . . . for several hours.

Evelyn Ciolfe
Xi Beta Xi, Lemon Grove, California

SAUCY SWEET POTATOES

1 16-oz. can sweet potatoes, drained
1/4 tsp. salt
1 8-oz. can applesauce
1/4 c. packed brown sugar
1/4 tsp. cinnamon
2 tbsp. butter

Layer . . . . . all ingredients in order given in 1-quart casserole.
Bake . . . . . . at 375 degrees for 30 to 35 minutes or until bubbly.

Del Campbell
Xi Epsilon, Oklahoma City, Oklahoma

CASSEROLE ONION BREAD

1 c. milk, scalded
3 tbsp. sugar
1 1/2 tbsp. butter
1 pkg. yeast
1 env. dry onion soup mix
4 c. flour

Combine . . . milk, sugar and butter in bowl; cool to lukewarm.
Dissolve . . . yeast in 3/4 cup warm water.
Stir . . . . into milk mixture with soup and flour.
Mix . . . . for 2 minutes.
Let . . . . rise, covered, until doubled in bulk.
Beat . . . . . . dough down for 1/2 minute.
Place . . . . . . in greased 1 1/2-quart casserole.
Bake . . . . . . at 375 degrees for 1 hour.

Toni Bell
Xi Eta Xi, Merritt Island, Florida

CHOCOLATE ECLAIR

2 pkg. vanilla instant pudding mix
2 c. milk
1 8-oz. carton whipped topping
1 box. graham crackers
1 can milk chocolate icing

Combine . . . pudding mix with milk in bowl, mixing well.
Fold . . . . . . in whipped topping.
Layer . . . . . graham crackers and pudding mixture alternately in 8 x 13-inch dish until all ingredients are used, beginning and ending with crackers.
Top . . . . with icing.
Chill . . . . . . overnight.
Yields . . . . . 18 servings.

Marie Wyatt
Xi Alpha Kappa, Hazelwood, North Carolina

Cheese Crispies
BSP Desserts & Party Foods, p. 70
Tomato Refresher
Baby Sitter's Tuna Casserole
Hot Fruit Casserole
Layered Carrot Casserole
Asparagus Au Gratin
Favorite Banana Bread
Raisin Chews
BSP Desserts & Party Foods, p. 97
Frozen Fruit Cup
BSP Desserts & Party Foods, p. 27

Parents' Night Out

TOMATO REFRESHER

2 qt. tomato juice
2 c. orange juice
1/4 c. lemon juice
1 tsp. celery salt
1 tbsp. Worcestershire sauce
3 tbsp. sugar
1 clove of garlic, minced

Combine ... all ingredients in 2 1/2-quart pitcher, mixing well.
Chill ...... covered, for several hours.
Yields ..... 12 servings.

Beverly Christian
Preceptor Laureate Alpha, Roseburg, Oregon

BABY SITTER'S TUNA CASSEROLE

1 can cream of mushroom soup
1 tbsp. instant minced onion
1/2 tsp. each oregano, salt
1   1-lb. can cut green beans
2 cans oil-pack tuna
1 1/3 c. minute rice
2 tbsp. chopped pimento

Combine ... soup, onion and seasonings in saucepan.
Drain ..... green beans, reserving liquid.
Add ...... enough water to reserved liquid to measure 1 1/4 cups.
Stir .... into soup mixture with tuna.
Bring ..... to a boil, stirring occasionally.
Stir .... in rice.
Pour ...... into casserole.
Arrange .... green beans around edge and pimento in center.
Bake ...... at 400 degrees for 20 minutes.
Garnish .... with Parmesan cheese before serving.
Yields ..... 4 servings.

Photograph for this recipe above.

HOT FRUIT CASSEROLE

1   20-oz. can pineapple rings, drained
1   29-oz. can each pear, peach
    halves, drained
1 jar spiced apple rings, drained
1/2 jar maraschino cherries
1 c. sugar
1/2 c. flour
1/2 c. pineapple juice
1 stick margarine
1/2 c. Sherry

Layer ..... fruit in 9 x 13-inch casserole.
Combine ... next 4 ingredients in saucepan.
Cook ...... over medium heat until margarine melts,
    stirring constantly.
Stir .... in Sherry.
Pour ...... over fruit.
Marinate ... in refrigerator for 24 hours.
Bake ...... at 350 degrees for 40 minutes.
Yields ..... 12-15 servings.

June Turner
Xi Alpha Eta, Mauldin, South Carolina

LAYERED CARROT CASSEROLE

3 tbsp. flour
3 tbsp. melted butter
1 1/2 c. milk
1 1/2 c. grated American cheese
4 c. cooked sliced carrots
1 can French-fried onion rings

Blend ..... flour into butter in saucepan.
Stir .... in milk gradually.
Cook ...... until thick, stirring constantly.
Add ...... cheese.
Cook ...... until cheese melts, stirring constantly.
Layer ..... carrots, cheese sauce and onion rings
    alternately in 1 1/2-quart casserole, re-
    serving 1/3 of the onion rings for
    topping.
Bake ...... at 350 degrees for 15 minutes.
Sprinkle ... crushed onion rings over top.
Bake ...... for 5 minutes longer.
Yields ..... 10 servings.

Nell Springer
Preceptor Alpha Delta, Columbia, Tennessee

ASPARAGUS AU GRATIN

3 tbsp. flour
Salt and pepper to taste
3 tbsp. butter, melted
1 1/2 c. milk
1 c. shredded Cheddar cheese
3 lg. cans asparagus tips, drained
2 cans sliced mushrooms
6 hard-boiled eggs, sliced
Bread crumbs
Paprika

Blend ..... flour, salt and pepper into butter in
    saucepan.
Stir .... in milk gradually.
Cook ...... until thick, stirring constantly.
Add ...... cheese.
Cook ...... until cheese melts, stirring constantly.
Layer ..... asparagus, mushrooms and eggs in but-
    tered casserole.
Cover ..... with sauce.
Sprinkle ... bread crumbs and paprika on top.
Bake ...... at 350 degrees for 20 to 30 minutes.
Yields ..... 8-10 servings.

Marlene Koenig
Xi Theta Nu, Ironton, Ohio

FAVORITE BANANA BREAD

1 c. sugar
1/2 c. margarine, softened
2 eggs
1 tsp. vanilla extract
1/2 c. sour cream
1/2 c. nuts
2 mashed bananas
1 1/2 c. flour
1 tsp. soda
1/2 tsp. salt

Cream ..... sugar and margarine in bowl for 2
    minutes.
Beat ...... in eggs and vanilla.
Add ...... sour cream and nuts, mixing well.
Stir .... in bananas, flour, soda and salt.
Pour ...... into greased and floured loaf pan.
Bake ...... at 350 degrees for 1 hour.

Patricia Stroshane
Preceptor Alpha Iota, Medford, Oregon

Garden Relish
Salmon Tetrazzini
Seven-Layer Salad
Tomato Aspic
Artichoke Casserole
Squash Delight
Italian Cheese Puffs
BSP Desserts & Party Foods, p. 72
Mousse Au Chocolat
Peanut Crunch Bar Cookies
BSP Desserts & Party Foods, p. 100

After The Concert

GARDEN RELISH

1 lg. head cauliflower, separated into flowerets
4 carrots, peeled, cut in 2-in. strips
2 c. 1-inch celery stalks
2 green peppers, cut in 2-in. strips
2 8-oz. jars pimento strips
1 1/2 c. wine vinegar
1 c. oil
1 tsp. each salt, oregano
4 tbsp. sugar
1/2 tsp. pepper

Combine ... all ingredients with 1/2 cup water in large pan.
Bring ...... to a boil, stirring occasionally.
Simmer .... covered, for 5 minutes; cool.
Chill ...... for 24 hours or longer.
Drain ..... well before serving.
Yields ..... 20 servings.

Bonnie Fox
Xi Mu Delta, Atwater, California

ELEGANT ARTICHOKE CASSEROLE

1 can artichoke hearts, drained, sliced
*   into halves*
3 hard-boiled eggs, sliced
1/2 c. sliced stuffed olives
1/4 c. sliced water chestnuts
1/2 c. grated American cheese
1 can mushroom soup
1/4 c. milk
1/2 c. buttered bread crumbs

Arrange .... artichokes in casserole.
Layer ..... eggs, olives, water chestnuts and cheese over artichokes.
Dilute ..... soup with milk in small bowl.
Pour ...... over layers.
Top .... with crumbs.
Bake ...... at 350 degrees until brown and bubbly.
Yields ..... 8 servings.

Emmie Lou Sheffield
Laureate Gamma, Mobile, Alabama

SALMON TETRAZZINI

1   1-lb. can salmon
Milk
2 tbsp. butter, melted
2 tbsp. flour
1/2 tsp. salt
Dash each of pepper, nutmeg
1 tbsp. Sherry
2 c. cooked spaghetti
1   4-oz. can sliced mushrooms, drained
2 tbsp. Parmesan cheese
2 tbsp. dry bread crumbs

Drain . . . . . salmon, reserving liquid.
Add . . . . . . enough milk to reserved liquid to mea-
sure 2 cups.
Blend . . . . butter, flour and seasonings in saucepan.
Stir . . . . in milk mixture gradually.
Cook . . . . . . until thick, stirring constantly.
Blend . . . . . in Sherry.
Mix . . . . half the sauce with spaghetti and mush-
rooms in greased 2-quart casserole.
Stir . . . . salmon into remaining sauce.
Spoon . . . . . into center of spaghetti.
Sprinkle . . . with cheese and crumbs.
Bake . . . . . . at 350 degrees for 25 to 30 minutes or
until bubbly.
Garnish . . . . with watercress.
Yields . . . . . 6 servings.

Photograph for this recipe on page 25.

SEVEN-LAYER SALAD

Shredded lettuce
1/2 c. chopped onions
1/2 c. sliced celery
1 pkg. frozen peas
1 jar mayonnaise
1 c. shredded Swiss cheese
6 slices crisp-cooked bacon

Layer . . . . . all ingredients in order listed into glass
bowl.
Chill . . . . . . for 6 hours or longer.

Gloria Odiorne
Kappa, Lewiston, Maine

TOMATO ASPIC

1 pkg. lemon gelatin
1 can tomato soup
Juice of 1/2 lemon
Salt and pepper
Dash of Worcestershire sauce

Dissolve . . . gelatin in 1 cup boiling water in bowl.
Stir . . . . in remaining ingredients.

Chill . . . . . . until firm.
Yields . . . . . 6 servings.

May add ingredients such as avocado, celery, artichoke
hearts, crab or shrimp as desired when gelatin is partially set.

June Willey
Preceptor Zeta Phi, Sunnyvale, California

SQUASH DELIGHT

2 1/2 lb. yellow squash, chopped
1 med. onion, chopped
1/2 stick margarine
1 can cream of chicken soup
1 c. sour cream
1/2 pkg. corn bread stuffing mix

Combine . . . squash and onion with a small amount of
water in saucepan.
Cook . . . . . . until tender; drain.
Add . . . . . . remaining ingredients, mixing well.
Spoon . . . . into casserole.
Bake . . . . . . at 350 degrees for 30 minutes.
Yields . . . . . 10-12 servings.

Laverne Lutringer
Preceptor Beta Sigma, Wharton, Texas

MOUSSE AU CHOCOLAT

1 sm. package semisweet chocolate chips
1/3 c. hot brewed coffee
4 eggs, separated
2 tbsp. Brandy
3 tbsp. sugar

Combine . . . chocolate chips and coffee in blender
container.
Process . . . . for 30 seconds or until smooth.
Add . . . . . . egg yolks and Brandy.
Process . . . . for 30 seconds.
Beat . . . . . . egg whites until soft peaks form; add
sugar gradually, beating until stiff.
Fold . . . . . . in chocolate mixture.
Spoon . . . . . into parfait glasses.
Chill . . . . . . for 1 hour or longer.
Garnish . . . . with whipped cream.
Yields . . . . . 4 servings.

Jean Schwabe
Theta Eta, Swainsboro, Georgia

*Winter One-Dish Dinner
or Fruited Chicken Curry
Cinnamon Apple Salad
Party Broccoli Casserole
Stuffed Zucchini
Spinach and Rice Casserole
Strawberry Pizza
BSP Desserts & Party Foods, p. 110
Lemon Custard Bars
BSP Desserts & Party Foods, p. 99*

First Snow of the Season

PARTY BROCCOLI CASSEROLE

*3 pkg. frozen chopped broccoli, cooked, drained
1 sm. jar chopped pimentos
1 4 1/2-oz. can mushroom pieces
1 can cream of mushroom soup
1 sm. carton sour cream
Bread crumbs
3 tbsp. butter, melted
Cheese, grated*

Combine ... first 4 ingredients in casserole.
Stir .... in sour cream.
Mix .... bread crumbs with butter in bowl.
Sprinkle ... over broccoli with cheese.
Bake ...... at 350 degrees for 1/2 hour.

*Sharon Ingram
Xi Zeta Zeta, St. Petersburg, Florida*

SPINACH AND RICE CASSEROLE

*1 box frozen chopped spinach, cooked,
    drained
1 c. rice, cooked
1 tsp. finely grated onion
1/4 lb. sharp Cheddar cheese,
    grated
4 tbsp. butter*

Combine ... spinach and rice with remaining ingredients in bowl, mixing well.
Spoon ..... into buttered 3-quart casserole.
Bake ...... at 275 degrees for 20 minutes or until bubbly.
Yields ..... 6 servings.

*Mary Lou Walsh
Xi Gamma Chi, Fayetteville, New York*

WINTER ONE-DISH DINNER

1 lb. stew meat
1 tbsp. oil
1 env. French's Spaghetti Sauce Mix
1 6-oz. can tomato paste
4 carrots, cut into chunks
1 10-oz. package frozen peas
1/2 c. sliced celery
2/3 c. French's Country-Style Mashed
*   Potato Flakes*
1 egg, beaten
1 tbsp. minced onion
1/2 c. flour
2 tsp. baking powder

Brown . . . . . stew meat in oil in skillet.
Stir . . . . in sauce mix, tomato paste and 2 cups water.
Simmer . . . . covered, for 30 minutes.
Add . . . . . . carrots.
Cook . . . . . covered, for 30 minutes longer.
Stir . . . . in peas and celery.
Bring . . . . . . to a boil.
Prepare . . . . potato flakes using package directions for 2 servings.
Stir . . . . in egg, onion and sifted dry ingredients.
Drop . . . . . . by spoonfuls onto stew.
Simmer . . . . tightly covered for 15 minutes.
Yields . . . . . 4 servings.

Photograph for this recipe on page 27.

FRUITED CHICKEN CURRY

6 lg. chicken breast halves, skinned, boned,
*   cut into chunks*
3 tbsp. cornstarch
3 med. onions, sliced
3 to 4 tsp. curry powder
1/4 c. melted butter
1/2 c. each apricot, pineapple liquid
1 can condensed chicken broth
1 1/2 tsp. salt
1/4 tsp. ginger
1 30-oz. can apricot halves, drained
1 15 1/4-oz. can pineapple chunks, drained
3 c. hot cooked rice

Combine . . . chicken and cornstarch in bowl, tossing to coat.
Saute . . . . . with onions and curry powder in butter in skillet for ten minutes or until onions are tender, stirring occasionally.
Stir . . . . in fruit liquids, broth, salt and ginger.
Cook . . . . . . until thickened and bubbly, stirring constantly.
Pour . . . . . . into 2-quart baking dish.
Top . . . . with apricots and pineapple.
Chill . . . . . . covered, in refrigerator.

Bake . . . . . . uncovered, at 350 degrees for 45 minutes or until hot and bubbly.
Serve . . . . . . with rice and chutney, raisins, toasted almonds and toasted coconut.
Yields . . . . . 4 servings.

Photograph for this recipe on page 4.

CINNAMON APPLE SALAD

3/4 c. red cinnamon candy
2 3-oz. packages lemon gelatin
1 1/2 c. tart applesauce
1 8-oz. package cream cheese, softened
1/2 c. mayonnaise
3/4 c. chopped celery
3/4 c. chopped nuts

Dissolve . . . candy in 3 cups boiling water in bowl.
Add . . . . . . gelatin, stirring until dissolved.
Stir . . . . in applesauce.
Pour . . . . . . half the gelatin mixture into 9 x 12-inch dish.
Chill . . . . . . until set.
Combine . . . remaining ingredients and remaining gelatin mixture in bowl, mixing well.
Pour . . . . . . over congealed layer.
Chill . . . . . . until firm.
Yields . . . . . 8 servings.

Martha E. Hardy
Preceptor Eta, Silver Spring, Maryland

STUFFED ZUCCHINI

3 med. zucchini
2 c. soft bread crumbs
1/2 c. Parmesan cheese
1 sm. onion, minced
2 tbsp. minced parsley
1/2 tsp. salt
2 eggs, beaten
Dash of pepper
Parmesan cheese to taste
2 tbsp. butter

Slice . . . . . . ends from zucchini.
Cook . . . . . . in boiling salted water in saucepan for 5 minutes; drain.
Cut . . . . zucchini in half lengthwise, removing and reserving pulp.
Combine . . . reserved pulp with remaining ingredients except butter.
Spoon . . . . . into zucchini shells.
Dot . . . . with butter and sprinkle with cheese.
Bake . . . . . . at 350 degrees for 1/2 hour.
Yields . . . . . 6 servings.

Joyce D. Quire
Xi Alpha Theta, Frankfort, Kentucky

Salmon-Dill Salad
with Pasta Shells
BSP All-Occasion Casseroles, p. 86
or D. J.'s Praise Pizza
Unusual Green Beans
Baked Pineapple
Zucchini Au Gratin
Layered Ham and Vegetable Casserole
Jewish Apple Cake
Chocolate Sponge
with Cointreau Sauce
BSP Desserts & Party Foods, p. 107
Florida Party Punch
BSP Desserts & Party Foods, p. 52

Neighbors' Progressive Dinner

D. J.'S PRAISE PIZZA

1 lb. sausage
1 4-oz. can mushrooms,
  drained
5 lg. flour tortillas
1/2 can pizza sauce
1 12-oz. package shredded mozzarella
  cheese

Brown . . . . . sausage and mushrooms in skillet; drain.
Chop . . . . . . sausage and mushrooms very fine.
Layer . . . . . tortillas, pizza sauce, sausage mixture and cheese alternately in casserole until all ingredients are used.
Bake . . . . . . at 350 degrees for 30 minutes.

Cathy Chatfield
Mu Gamma, Manitoba Beach, Michigan

UNUSUAL GREEN BEANS

3 pkg. frozen French-style green beans
1   5-oz. can water chestnuts, drained, sliced
2 cans cream of celery soup
1/2 c. milk
1/8 tsp. pepper
1   8-oz. package frozen French-fried onion rings

Cook . . . . . green beans according to package direc-
tions for 4 minutes; drain.
Layer . . . . . beans and water chestnuts in greased
2-quart casserole.
Blend . . . . . soup, milk and pepper in bowl.
Pour . . . . . over water chestnuts.
Bake . . . . . . at 375 degrees for 25 minutes.
Spread . . . . onion rings on baking sheet.
Bake . . . . . . for 15 minutes, turning once.
Arrange . . . . onion rings around edge of casserole be-
fore serving.

Photograph for this recipe on page 29.

BAKED PINEAPPLE

1   16-oz. can pineapple chunks
1 c. sugar
2 tbsp. flour
1 c. grated Cheddar cheese
1 c. bread crumbs
3 tbsp. margarine

Drain . . . . . pineapple, reserving juice.
Blend . . . . . sugar, flour and reserved juice in
saucepan.
Cook . . . . . . until thick, stirring constantly.
Combine . . . pineapple and cheese in 8-inch square
baking dish.
Spoon . . . . . sauce over pineapple mixture.
Top . . . . with crumbs.
Dot . . . . with margarine.
Bake . . . . . . at 350 degrees for 25 to 30 minutes or
until lightly browned.

Velda Kloke
Xi Gamma Zeta, Harvard, Nebraska

ZUCCHINI AU GRATIN

4 med. zucchini, sliced 1/4-in. thick
1 clove of garlic, minced
1 sm. onion, chopped
4 tbsp. oil
1/2 tsp. salt
1/4 tsp. pepper
2 tbsp. Parmesan cheese
1/4 c. tomato sauce
2 or 3 slices Swiss cheese

Saute . . . . . zucchini, garlic and onion in oil in skillet
for 5 minutes.

Sprinkle . . . with salt, pepper and Parmesan cheese.
Place . . . . . . in 1-quart casserole.
Brush . . . . . with tomato sauce.
Top . . . . with Swiss cheese.
Bake . . . . . . at 350 degrees for 15 to 20 minutes or
until cheese melts.

Lila Warrell
Preceptor Upsilon, Muncie, Indiana

LAYERED HAM AND VEGETABLE CASSEROLE

5 c. shredded cabbage
2 c. chopped cooked ham
1 apple, peeled, chopped
Chopped onion to taste
Salt and pepper to taste
2 tbsp. butter, softened
1/2 c. milk

Layer . . . . . half the cabbage, ham, apple, onion, salt
and pepper in 2-quart casserole; repeat
layers.
Top . . . . with butter and milk.
Bake . . . . . . at 350 degrees for 40 to 45 minutes.
Yields . . . . . 6 servings.

Lois Maurer
Preceptor Laureate Delta, Jefferson City, Missouri

JEWISH APPLE CAKE

2 3/4 c. sugar
3 c. flour
3 tsp. baking powder
1 c. oil
4 eggs, beaten
1/3 c. orange juice
2 1/2 tsp. vanilla extract
2 tsp. cinnamon
5 lg. apples, sliced

Combine . . . 2 cups sugar and next 6 ingredients in
mixer bowl.
Beat . . . . . . for 10 minutes.
Mix . . . . 3/4 cup sugar and cinnamon in small
bowl.
Layer . . . . . batter, apples and cinnamon mixture
alternately in tube pan until all ingredients are used, ending with apples and
cinnamon mixture.
Bake . . . . . . at 350 degrees for 1 to 1 1/4 hours or
until cake tests done.
Cool . . . . . . for 1 hour or longer before removing
from pan.
Garnish . . . . with sprinkle of confectioners' sugar.

Teresa Schafer
Xi Alpha Pi, Hagerstown, Maryland

Scalloped Eggs and Ham
or Company Crab Casseroles
Nut-Wiches
Lima Bean Casserole Deluxe
Italian Broccoli Casserole
Celery-Mushroom Casserole
Chocolate-Cherry Cake
BSP Desserts & Party Foods, p. 83
Orange Angel Cream
BSP Desserts & Party Foods, p. 108
Ginger Lime Punch
BSP Desserts & Party Foods, p. 53

Campaign Supper

SCALLOPED EGGS AND HAM

1 1/2 tbsp. chopped onion
2/3 c. margarine,
melted
1 c. sifted flour
1 tbsp. salt
1 1/2 tsp. dry mustard
1/8 tsp. pepper
7 c. hot milk
1/2 tsp. Worcestershire sauce
18 hard-boiled eggs,
chopped

5 c. diced smoked ham
2 tbsp. chopped parsley

Saute . . . . . onion in margarine in skillet until tender.
Blend . . . . . in flour and next 3 seasonings.
Stir . . . . into hot milk in large soup pot gradually.
Cook . . . . . . until thick, stirring constantly.
Stir . . . . in remaining ingredients.
Pour . . . . . . into large baking pan.
Bake . . . . . . at 425 degrees for 25 minutes.
Yields . . . . . 16 servings.

Photograph for this recipe above.

COMPANY CRAB CASSEROLES

1 10-oz. can frozen condensed cream of
   shrimp soup
1/4 c. bean liquid
1 7 1/2-oz. can crab meat, rinsed, flaked
1 16-oz. can green beans, drained
1/4 c. finely chopped celery
2 tbsp. Sherry
1/2 tsp. lemon juice
1/4 tsp. each basil, tarragon
3/4 c. soft bread crumbs
2 tbsp. butter, melted
2 tbsp. grated Parmesan cheese

Heat ...... soup with liquid in saucepan until soup
          thaws, stirring constantly.
Add ...... crab meat, beans, celery, Sherry, lemon
          juice and herbs, mixing well.
Spoon ..... into buttered individual casseroles.
Combine ... bread crumbs and butter in bowl.
Sprinkle ... around edges of casseroles.
Dust ...... with cheese.
Bake ...... at 350 degrees for 20 minutes.
Yields ..... 4-5 servings.

Photograph for this recipe on page 2.

NUT-WICHES

2 8-oz. packages cream cheese, softened
2 c. finely chopped nuts
1 c. drained crushed pineapple
1/4 c. finely chopped green pepper
2 tbsp. chopped onion
Whole wheat and white bread slices, trimmed

Combine ... first 5 ingredients in bowl, mixing well.
Spread .... on bread.
Cut .... bread into fourths.

Louise Palmer
Preceptor Delta Mu, Amarillo, Texas

LIMA BEAN CASSEROLE DELUXE

1 tsp. prepared mustard
1 tsp. Worcestershire sauce
1/2 tsp. lemon juice
3/4 c. mayonnaise
1 can water chestnuts, drained, chopped
1 sm. onion, chopped
1 10-oz. package frozen lima beans,
   cooked, drained
1 16-oz. can English peas, drained
1 c. buttered cracker crumbs

Blend ..... first 4 ingredients in bowl.
Stir .... in remaining ingredients except crumbs.

Spoon ..... into 2-quart casserole.
Top .... with crumbs.
Bake ...... at 350 degrees for 45 minutes.

Bernice Cole
Preceptor Nu, Anniston, Alabama

ITALIAN BROCCOLI CASSEROLE

2 eggs, beaten
1 can Cheddar cheese soup
1/2 tsp. oregano
3 tbsp. Parmesan cheese
1 8-oz. can stewed tomatoes
2 10-oz. packages frozen chopped broccoli,
   cooked, drained

Combine ... first 4 ingredients in bowl, mixing well.
Stir .... in tomatoes and broccoli.
Turn ...... into 6 x 10-inch baking dish.
Top .... with cheese.
Bake ...... at 350 degrees for 30 minutes.

Brenda Benedict
Beta Nu, Encampment, Wyoming

CELERY-MUSHROOM CASSEROLE

3 c. 1/2-inch celery slices
1/2 tsp. salt
1/2 c. sliced mushrooms
Butter
1 can peas, drained
1 can cream of mushroom soup
1/2 c. grated American cheese
Buttered cracker crumbs

Steam ..... celery with 1/2 teaspoon salt in steamer
          for 10 minutes; drain.
Saute ..... mushrooms in a small amount of butter
          in skillet.
Add ...... celery, peas and 1/2 can soup, mixing
          well.
Spoon ..... half the mixture into greased casserole.
Layer ..... 1/4 cup cheese, remaining celery mix-
          ture, soup and cheese on top.
Top .... with crumbs.
Bake ...... at 350 degrees for 30 minutes or until
          brown and bubbly.

Marilyn Beaver
Preceptor Eta Omega, Piedmont, California

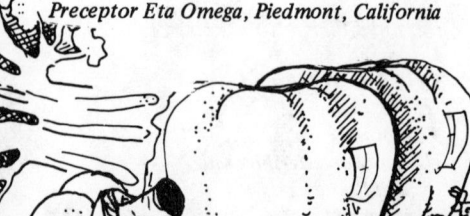

Beef & Veal

BEEF CURRY IN A HURRY

1/2 c. chopped onion
1 clove of garlic, minced
3 tbsp. melted butter
1 1/2 lb. boneless beef, cut into
*   1/2-in. cubes*
1 to 1 1/2 tbsp. curry powder
1 tsp. salt
1/2 c. golden raisins
1 tbsp. flour
1 med. apple, peeled, sliced
1   10-oz. package frozen peas and
*   carrots, thawed*
1   10-oz. package corn bread mix
1 c. Cheddar cheese cubes

Saute . . . . . . onion and garlic in butter in skillet until tender.
Add . . . . beef.
Cook . . . . until brown.
Stir . . . . in curry powder and salt blended with 1 1/2 cups water and raisins.
Simmer . . . . . covered, for 20 minutes or until beef is tender.
Stir . . . . in flour blended with 1/4 cup water.
Bring . . . . to a boil, stirring constantly.
Add . . . . apple.
Spoon . . . . . . into 2-quart casserole.
Arrange . . . . . peas and carrots over top.
Prepare . . . . . corn bread using package directions.
Fold . . . . in cheese.
Spread . . . . . over casserole.
Bake . . . . at 425 degrees for 12 to 15 minutes.
Serve . . . . with strawberry yogurt.
Yields . . . . . . 8 servings.

Photograph for this recipe on page 33.

AFRICAN CHOW MEIN

3/4 lb. each beef, pork, cubed
1 lg. onion, chopped
2 c. chopped celery
2 cans each cream of chicken, cream of
*   mushroom soup*
1 lg. can mushrooms
1/4 c. soy sauce
1 c. slivered almonds
1 c. rice

Brown . . . . . . pork and beef with onion in skillet.
Combine . . . . with remaining ingredients and 2 soup cans hot water in large casserole.
Bake . . . . covered, in moderate oven until meat and rice are tender.
Yields . . . . . . 15 servings.

Vera W. Stahl
Alpha Delta, Hettinger, North Dakota

BEEF CASSEROLE STEW

2 1/2 to 3 lb. beef chuck, cubed
4 med. potatoes, peeled, quartered
6 med. carrots, cut into lg. pieces
3 stalks celery, cut into lg. pieces
3 med. onions, quartered
1/4 c. flour
1/4 c. each soy sauce, dry Sherry
1/2 tsp. each salt, pepper
1 or 2 green peppers, cut into lg. pieces

Layer . . . . . . beef, potatoes, carrots, celery and onions alternately in 3-quart casserole until all ingredients are used, sprinkling with flour between each layer.
Mix . . . . soy sauce, Sherry, salt and pepper in bowl.
Pour . . . . over layers.
Bake . . . . covered, at 300 degrees for 2 to 2 1/2 hours or until beef is tender.
Top . . . . with green peppers.
Bake . . . . for 20 minutes longer or until peppers are tender-crisp.
Yields . . . . . . 6-8 servings.

Nell Walker
Xi Alpha Phi, Indianapolis, Indiana

BEEF-PEPPER AND BEAN CASSEROLE

2 lb. beef chuck, cubed
1/4 c. flour
1 tsp. salt
Dash of pepper
3/4 tsp. ginger
1/4 c. oil
1 tsp. chili sauce
1 tsp. chili powder
1   8-oz. can tomatoes

2 1/2 tbsp. brown sugar
3 tbsp. wine vinegar
1 1/2 tbsp. Worcestershire sauce
2 med. cloves of garlic, minced
1 bay leaf
1 c. sliced mushrooms
1 16-oz. can kidney beans, drained
1 med. green pepper, sliced

Coat . . . . beef with flour seasoned with salt, pepper and ginger.
Brown . . . . . . in oil in skillet.
Mix . . . . remaining ingredients except beans and green pepper in bowl.
Combine . . . . with beef in 2-quart casserole, mixing well.
Bake . . . . covered, at 325 degrees for 1 1/2 hours.
Stir . . . . in kidney beans and green pepper.
Bake . . . . for 30 minutes longer or until beef is tender.
Yields . . . . . . 6 servings.

Jerry Olson
Xi Omega, Memphis, Tennessee

EASY BEEF DISH

2 lb. stew beef, cubed
1 pkg. dry onion soup mix
2 c. Burgundy
1 can golden mushroom soup

Combine . . . . all ingredients with 1/2 soup can water in 2-quart casserole, mixing well.
Bake . . . . covered, at 325 degrees for 3 hours.
Serve . . . . over noodles.
Yields . . . . . . 6 servings.

Norma Anderson
Beta Sigma Phi XP 1533, Troy, Illinois

HUNTER STEW

6 slices bacon, cut into 1-in. pieces
1 lg. onion, chopped
1/2 lb. each beef, pork, cubed
1/2 lb. Polish sausage, sliced
2 c. beef broth
1 6-oz. can sliced mushrooms
1/2 c. dry white wine
1 tsp. paprika
1/2 tsp. salt

1 bay leaf
2 16-oz. cans chopped sauerkraut, drained

Cook . . . . bacon with onion in large soup pot until bacon is crisp; drain and set aside, reserving 2 tablespoons drippings.
Brown . . . . . . beef and pork in reserved drippings in skillet.
Stir . . . . in bacon mixture and remaining ingredients except sauerkraut.
Simmer . . . . . for 1 1/2 to 2 hours or until beef and pork are tender.
Add . . . . sauerkraut, mixing well.
Cook . . . . until heated through; remove bay leaf.
Yields . . . . . . 10 servings.

Katherine Logan
Laureate Alpha, Anchorage, Alaska

MY CASSEROLE

1 lb. stew beef cubes
1 onion, sliced
1 can beef consomme
1/2 c. red wine
1/4 c. flour

Layer . . . . . . all ingredients in casserole in order given.
Bake . . . . at 300 degrees for 3 hours.
Serve . . . . over rice.
Yields . . . . . . 4 servings.

Jane Koehn
Laureate Alpha Zeta, Jacksonville, Florida

SAVORY SHORT RIB DINNER

4 to 5 lb. short ribs
Garlic salt and pepper to taste
Monosodium glutamate
1 tsp. (rounded) instant beef bouillon

Place . . . . short ribs in single layer in 9 x 13-inch baking dish.
Sprinkle . . . . with seasonings.
Add . . . . bouillon dissolved in 1 1/4 cups hot water.
Bake . . . . covered, at 350 degrees for 2 hours or until tender.
Yields . . . . . . 4 servings.

Millie Maxwell
Xi Upsilon Xi, Rio Vista, California

MEAT AND RICE BAKE CASSEROLE

1 can mushroom soup
1/2 c. sour cream
1/2 c. milk
1 1/2 c. cubed cooked beef
1 1/2 c. cooked rice
1 c. canned peas, drained
1   2-oz. can chopped mushrooms, drained
1 tbsp. chopped parsley
3/4 c. soft bread crumbs
1 tbsp. melted butter

Combine .... soup, sour cream and milk in bowl, mixing well.
Stir .... in next 5 ingredients.
Pour .... into 1 1/2-quart casserole.
Toss .... crumbs with butter in bowl.
Sprinkle .... over beef mixture.
Bake .... at 350 degrees for 55 to 60 minutes or until bubbly.
Yields ...... 4-6 servings.

Sonia Vadraska
Xi Epsilon Theta, Wilson, Kansas

OVEN BEEF STEW

1 lb. stew beef, cubed
3 carrots, cut into lg. pieces
3 stalks celery, cut into lg. pieces
3 onions, quartered
1 sm. can tomato sauce
1 bay leaf
Pinch of marjoram
3 tbsp. Minute tapioca
Salt to taste
Potatoes, sliced (opt.)

Combine .... all ingredients with 1 cup water in casserole, mixing well.
Bake .... covered, at 275 degrees for 5 hours or until beef is tender.
Yields ...... 4-6 servings.

Millie Neel
Preceptor Gamma Sigma, Sarasota, Florida

SIRLOIN TIP CASSEROLE

1 lb. sirloin tip, cubed
1 c. chopped onion
2 c. chopped celery
1 can each mushroom, beefy
*   mushroom soup*

2 tbsp. soy sauce
2/3 c. rice

Brown ...... sirloin tip with onion and celery in a small amount of oil in Dutch oven, stirring frequently.
Add .... remaining 4 ingredients with 2 cups water, mixing well.
Bake .... covered, at 300 degrees for 1 1/2 hours.
Yields ...... 6-8 servings.

Marge Pickett
Xi Epsilon, Oklahoma City, Oklahoma

STEAK AND ONION PIE

1 c. sliced onion
Shortening
1 lb. round steak, cubed
1 1/4 c. flour
2 1/2 tsp. salt
1/8 tsp. paprika
Dash each of allspice, ginger
2 c. chopped potatoes
1 egg, slightly beaten

Saute ...... onion in 1/4 cup shortening in skillet; remove.
Coat .... steak with flour seasoned with 2 teaspoons salt, paprika, allspice and ginger.
Brown ...... steak in pan drippings.
Add .... 2 1/2 cups boiling water.
Simmer ..... covered, for 1 hour or until tender.
Add .... potatoes.
Cook .... for 10 minutes longer.
Spoon ...... into greased 8-inch casserole.
Top .... with sauteed onion.
Combine .... 1 cup flour and 1/2 teaspoon salt in bowl.
Cut .... in 1/3 cup shortening until crumbly.
Add .... egg, mixing well.
Roll .... into 8-inch circle on floured surface.
Cover ...... casserole, sealing edge and cutting several slits in top.
Bake .... at 450 degrees for 30 minutes.
Yields ...... 4-6 servings.

Peg Trost
Preceptor Alpha Theta, West Chester, Pennsylvania

OVEN BEEF STROGANOFF

2 lb. stew beef, cubed
1/4 c. flour
2 tbsp. oil
1 can cream of mushroom soup
1 pkg. stroganoff sauce mix
1 tbsp. instant minced onion
8 oz. sliced mushrooms
1/2 c. sour cream

Coat . . . . beef with flour.
Brown . . . . . . in oil in skillet.
Combine . . . . next 3 ingredients in bowl, mixing well.
Stir . . . . into skillet with mushrooms, adding water if necessary.
Spoon . . . . . . into 2-quart casserole.
Bake . . . . covered, at 350 degrees for 1 1/2 hours or until beef is tender.
Stir . . . . in sour cream.
Serve . . . . . . over noodles.
Yields . . . . . . 6 servings.

Dolores Kastello
Preceptor Nu, Waukesha, Wisconsin

CHUCK ROAST AND RICE

1   2 1/2 to 3-lb. boneless chuck roast
Flour.
1 med. onion, chopped
1 sm. green pepper, chopped
1 med. carrot, sliced
1 tbsp. oil
1 tsp. MSG
2 c. minute rice

Coat . . . . roast with flour.
Brown . . . . . . with onion, green pepper and carrot in oil in large skillet.
Add . . . . MSG and 1 cup water.
Simmer . . . . . covered, for 1 1/2 hours.
Remove . . . . roast and cut into bite-sized pieces.
Add . . . . roast and 1 1/4 cups water or more to skillet.
Bring . . . . to a boil.
Stir . . . . in rice.
Simmer . . . . . covered, for 12 to 15 minutes or until rice is tender.
Yields . . . . . . 6 servings.

Sandra Gribbin
Xi Delta Alpha, Bethlehem, Pennsylvania

BEEF AND ONIONS

2 tbsp. cornstarch
1/2 tsp. each salt, sugar
2 tbsp. each Sherry, soy sauce
1 lb. beef, cut into thin strips
2 lg. onions, chopped
1 can sliced mushrooms
1 green pepper, sliced

Combine . . . . cornstarch, salt, sugar, Sherry and soy sauce in bowl, blending well.
Marinate . . . . beef in soy sauce mixture for 1 hour.
Brown . . . . . . in oil in skillet; remove beef from skillet.
Saute . . . . . . vegetables in pan drippings.
Return . . . . . beef to skillet with 1/2 cup water.
Simmer . . . . . covered, for several minutes, adding additional water if necessary.
Yields . . . . . . 2-3 servings.

Karen Krug
Kappa, Lewiston, Maine

CHINESE BEEF AND BEANS

1 env. gravy mix
1 tbsp. soy sauce
1/2 tsp. sugar
1/8 tsp. ginger
1 lb. round steak, cut into thin strips
1   10-oz. package frozen French-style green beans, thawed
3 tbsp. oil
2 c. cooked rice

Mix . . . . first 4 ingredients in bowl.
Add . . . . beef, tossing to coat.
Stir-fry . . . . . beans in half the oil in large skillet for 5 minutes or until tender-crisp; remove from skillet.
Add . . . . beef and remaining oil.
Stir-fry . . . . . for 3 to 5 minutes or to desired degree of doneness.
Stir . . . . in beans and 2/3 cup water.
Place . . . . rice in 2-quart casserole.
Top . . . . with beef mixture.
Bake . . . . at 350 degrees for 15 to 20 minutes, or until heated through.
Yields . . . . . . 4 servings.

Pat Boenker
Xi Zeta Alpha, Berea, Ohio

BEEF STROGANOFF

1 lb. round steak
3 tbsp. flour
1 tsp. each salt, paprika
1/4 tsp. pepper
1/8 tsp. garlic powder
1/4 c. butter
1/2 c. finely chopped onion
1 clove of garlic, minced (opt.)
1 can beef consomme
1 lb. mushrooms, sliced
1/2 c. sour cream
2 tbsp. chopped green onion

Pound . . . . . . steak to 1/4-inch thickness and cut into strips.
Combine . . . . flour and seasonings in bowl.
Coat . . . . steak with flour mixture.
Brown . . . . . . steak in butter in large skillet.
Add . . . . onion and garlic.
Cook . . . . until onion is transparent.
Add . . . . consomme and mushrooms, mixing well.
Simmer . . . . . covered, for 1 hour or until steak is tender, stirring occasionally and adding water, if necessary.
Stir . . . . in sour cream and green onion.
Serve . . . . over mashed potatoes.
Yields . . . . . . 4-6 servings.

Joan E. Sutton
Iota Gamma, Kincardine, Ontario, Canada

CHINESE PEPPER STEAK

1 1/2 lb. lean round steak, cut into 1/4-in. strips
1 tbsp. paprika
3 tbsp. butter
1 tsp. minced garlic
1 1/2 c. beef broth
1/2 lb. mushrooms, sliced
1 lg. green pepper, cut into strips
1 med. zucchini, sliced
1 c. sliced green onions
1 c. sliced celery
2 carrots, sliced
2 tbsp. cornstarch
1/4 c. soy sauce
1 6-oz. can sliced water chestnuts
2 lg. tomatoes, cut into 8 wedges
4 c. cooked rice

Season . . . . . beef with paprika.
Let . . . . stand for several minutes.
Brown . . . . . . beef in butter in large skillet, stirring frequently.
Add . . . . garlic and broth, mixing well.
Simmer . . . . . covered, for 30 minutes.
Stir . . . . in vegetables.
Cook . . . . covered, for 5 minutes.
Blend . . . . . . cornstarch, soy sauce and 1/4 cup water in bowl.
Stir . . . . into beef mixture.
Cook . . . . for 2 minutes or until thick, stirring constantly.
Add . . . . water chestnuts and tomatoes, mixing well.
Serve . . . . over rice.
Yields . . . . . . 6 servings.

Carol Sassin
Xi Psi Beta, Beeville, Texas

ORIENTAL BEEF AND PEA PODS

1 1/2 lb. sirloin steak, thinly sliced cross grain
1 can condensed consomme
3 tbsp. soy sauce
1/4 tsp. each ginger, Accent
1 bunch green onions, chopped
2 pkg. frozen pea pods, partially thawed
2 tbsp. cornstarch
1 can bean sprouts, rinsed, drained

Brown . . . . . . steak in large skillet; remove to warm place.
Mix . . . . consomme, soy sauce, ginger and Accent in bowl.
Add . . . . to skillet with onions and pea pods, mixing well.
Simmer . . . . . covered, for 3 minutes.
Mix . . . . cornstarch and 2 tablespoons cold water in small bowl.
Add . . . . to vegetables, stirring constantly.
Cook . . . . for 2 to 3 minutes or until thickened, stirring constantly.
Stir . . . . in browned steak and bean sprouts.
Cook . . . . until heated through.
Serve . . . . over rice.
Yields . . . . . . 6 servings.

Ellen L. Smith
Laureate Xi, Coldwater, Michigan

BAKED STEAK IN TOMATO SAUCE

2 lb. round steak, cut into
   serving-sized pieces
Salt and pepper
3 tbsp. oil
1 lg. onion, sliced
1 lg. mango, chopped (opt.)
1 6-oz. can tomato paste
1/4 c. flour
1/2 c. red wine
1 bay leaf
1/4 tsp. each thyme, sugar

Season ..... beef with salt and pepper to
     taste.
Brown ...... in oil in skillet.
Place .... in 2-quart casserole.
Top .... with onion and mango.
Combine .... remaining ingredients, 1/4 tea-
     spoon salt and 1/8 teaspoon pep-
     per in bowl, mixing well.
Pour .... over casserole.
Bake .... covered, at 350 degrees for 1 1/2
     hours.
Yields ...... 4-6 servings.

Bea Glassco
Iota Delta, La Place, Louisiana

CALDILLO MEXICAN STEW

1 2-lb. cube round steak
2 tbsp. shortening
1 med. onion, chopped
1 clove of garlic, minced
1/4 tsp. cumin
Salt and pepper to taste
6 chopped peeled green chilies
1 can stewed tomatoes, mashed
1 1/2 c. chopped potatoes

Brown ...... steak in shortening in large
     skillet.
Add .... next 5 ingredients.
Cook .... until onion is tender, stirring
     frequently.
Add .... chilies, tomatoes, potatoes and 3
     tomato cans water, mixing well.
Simmer ..... for 45 minutes.
Yields ...... 8-10 servings.

Dolores Rios
Xi Pi Pi, El Paso, Texas

SKILLET STEAK AND POTATOES

1 2-lb. round steak, tenderized
1/2 c. flour
1 tbsp. butter
4 c. chopped potatoes
1 med. onion, sliced
Salt and pepper to taste
1 can cream of mushroom soup

Coat .... steak with flour.
Brown ...... in butter in skillet.
Arrange ..... potatoes and onion over steak.
Season ..... with salt and pepper.
Mix .... soup and 1/2 cup water in
     saucepan.
Cook .... until heated through.
Pour .... over steak.
Simmer ..... covered, for 1 to 1 1/2 hours or
     until steak is tender.
Yields ...... 6 servings.

Judy Anderson
Iota Phi, West Bend, Iowa

SUNDAY-STYLE SWISS STEAK

2 tbsp. flour
1 1/2 tsp. salt
1/4 tsp. pepper
1 1 1/2-lb. 1-inch round steak, cut
   into 4 pieces
1 onion, sliced
3 tbsp. oil
2 cans tomato sauce
1 c. frozen mixed vegetables

Pound ...... flour seasoned with salt and pep-
     per into steak with meat mallet.
Cook .... onion in oil in skillet until
     golden brown; remove onion.
Brown ...... steak in pan drippings.
Spoon ...... onion over steaks.
Blend ...... 1 can tomato sauce with 1/2 cup
     water in bowl.
Pour .... over steak.
Simmer ..... covered, for 1 1/2 hours.
Add .... vegetables and remaining 1 can
     tomato sauce, mixing well.
Simmer ..... covered, for 25 minutes longer.
Yields ...... 4 servings.

Joyce Bears
Preceptor Phi, Denver, Colorado

SAUSAGE-STUFFED BEEF BIRDS

1/2 lb. sausage
1/4 c. each minced onion, celery
1/2 c. finely chopped apple
3 c. toasted bread cubes
1/2 tsp. salt
1 1/2 lb. round steak, 1/2 in. thick
1/2 c. flour
1/2 c. shortening
1 1/2 c. barbecue sauce

Brown . . . . . . sausage in skillet, stirring until crumbly; drain.
Add . . . . onion, celery and apple, mixing well.
Cook . . . . . . until onion is tender.
Add . . . . to bread crumbs with salt and 1/4 cup water in bowl, tossing lightly to mix.
Cut . . . . steak into 5 portions and pound to flatten.
Dredge . . . . . in flour.
Spoon . . . . . . sausage mixture into center of each steak, rolling to enclose filling; fasten with toothpicks.
Brown . . . . . . in shortening in Dutch oven; drain.
Cover . . . . . . with barbecue sauce.
Bake . . . . covered, at 325 degrees, for 2 hours.
Yields . . . . . . 5 servings.

Susan Schwartz
Epsilon Iota, Blair, Nebraska

BEEF AND SAUSAGE CASSEROLE

5 or 6 Italian sausage links, cut into bite-sized pieces
1 lb. lean stew beef, cut into bite-sized pieces
4 potatoes, quartered
1 can kidney beans
2 onions, sliced
4 carrots, sliced
1 tsp. basil
1/2 tsp. garlic powder
2 to 3 c. beef broth

Cook . . . . sausage in Dutch oven until lightly browned.
Add . . . . beef.
Cook . . . . until browned.
Add . . . . remaining ingredients, mixing well.

Bake . . . . at 350 degrees for 1 1/2 hours or until potatoes are tender.
Yields . . . . . . 4-6 servings.

Sherry G. Daley
Zeta Tau, Diamond Bar, California

FRIZZLED CHIPPED BEEF

1 lg. zucchini
1 3-oz. package smoked sliced beef, chopped
4 tbsp. butter, melted
3 tbsp. chopped onion
1/2 lb. fresh mushrooms, sliced
1 tbsp. lemon juice
1/4 c. flour
1 tsp. dry mustard
2 c. milk
1 8-oz. can water chestnuts, drained, quartered
2 tbsp. Sherry
2 tsp. Worcestershire sauce
1 c. shredded Cheddar cheese
6 tomato slices
2 tbsp. Parmesan cheese

Cut . . . . zucchini into thirds crosswise.
Boil . . . . in water in saucepan for 15 minutes or until tender-crisp; drain and set aside.
Saute . . . . . . smoked beef in 1 tablespoon butter in skillet until frizzled.
Add . . . . onion.
Cook . . . . for 1 minute, stirring constantly.
Stir . . . . in mushrooms and lemon juice.
Cook . . . . for several minutes, stirring occasionally.
Blend . . . . . . flour and mustard into 3 tablespoons butter in saucepan.
Cook . . . . over low heat until smooth.
Stir . . . . in milk.
Bring . . . . to a boil, stirring constantly.
Boil . . . . for 1 minute, stirring constantly; remove from heat.
Add . . . . beef mixture, water chestnuts, Sherry, Worcestershire sauce and cheese, stirring until cheese melts.
Cut . . . . each piece zucchini into 4 lengthwise slices.
Place . . . . in 6 buttered 8-ounce casseroles.
Pour . . . . 1/2 cup beef mixture into each casserole.

Top . . . . with tomato slices.
Bake . . . . at 350 degrees for 10 minutes.
Sprinkle . . . . with cheese.
Broil . . . . until lightly browned.
Yields . . . . . . 6 servings.

Photograph for this recipe above.

PHYLLIS' REUBEN CASSEROLE

1 16-oz. can sauerkraut, drained
1 12-oz. can corned beef, crumbled
2 c. shredded Swiss cheese
1/2 c. mayonnaise
1/4 c. Thousand Island dressing
2 med. tomatoes, sliced
1/4 c. bread crumbs
2 tbsp. butter, melted

Layer . . . . . . first 3 ingredients in order given
              in casserole.
Mix . . . . mayonnaise and salad dressing in
              bowl.
Spread . . . . . over cheese.
Top . . . . with tomatoes.
Mix . . . . bread crumbs with butter.
Sprinkle . . . . over tomatoes.
Bake . . . . at 325 degrees until heated
              through.

Phyllis Emmel
Phi Alpha Zeta, Jefferson City, Missouri

EASY CORNED BEEF CASSEROLE

1 12-oz. can corned beef, cubed
1 8-oz. package macaroni, cooked
1/4 lb. American cheese, cubed
1 can cream of chicken soup
1 c. milk
1/2 c. chopped onion
3/4 c. buttered bread crumbs

Combine . . . . first 6 ingredients in greased
              2-quart casserole.
Top . . . . with bread crumbs.
Bake . . . . at 350 degrees for 1 hour.

Barb Olson
Xi Upsilon, Missoula, Montana

CORNED BEEF-NOODLE DISH

1 12-oz. can corned beef, chopped
1 12-oz. package noodles, cooked
2 cans cream of mushroom soup
1 sm. jar pimentos, chopped
1 1/2 c. evaporated milk
Chopped onion to taste
1/4 lb. Cheddar cheese, grated
1 sm. bag potato chips, crushed

Combine . . . . first 6 ingredients in greased 9 x
              13-inch baking pan.
Top . . . . with cheese and potato chips.
Bake . . . . at 350 degrees for 1 hour or un-
              til brown.

Mary C. Sollazzo
Preceptor Beta Mu, Sioux City, Iowa

CHEESE-TOPPED CORNED BEEF CASSEROLE

1 c. elbow macaroni
1 pkg. dried corned beef, cut up
1 sm. can sliced mushrooms
1 can cream of mushroom soup
1 sm. onion, chopped
1 c. grated Cheddar cheese

Soak . . . . macaroni in cold water in bowl
              for 1 hour; drain.
Combine . . . . with next 4 ingredients in
              1 1/2-quart casserole, mixing
              well.
Top . . . . with cheese.
Bake . . . . at 350 degrees for 1 hour.

Carin Andrews
Lambda Sigma, Dayton, Ohio

CHINESE VEAL

1 lb. veal, cubed
2 tbsp. oil
1 c. finely chopped onion
1/2 c. rice
1 can chicken with rice soup
4 tbsp. soy sauce
1 c. finely chopped celery
1 pkg. frozen peas
1/4 c. toasted almonds

Brown . . . . . . veal in oil in skillet.
Add . . . . onion.
Saute . . . . . . until onion is golden.
Add . . . . 1 cup water and next 3 ingredients, mixing well.
Spoon . . . . . . into 2-quart casserole.
Bake . . . . covered, at 425 degrees for 40 minutes.
Stir . . . . in celery and peas.
Bake . . . . covered, for 20 minutes longer.
Sprinkle . . . . with almonds.
Yields . . . . . . 10-12 servings.

Ann Ross McClentic
Xi Theta Tau, Memphis, Missouri

FANTASTIC NOODLE HASH

1 1/2 lb. each veal, pork
1 lg. package fine noodles
3 carrots, grated
1 green pepper, chopped
1 lg. can mushrooms
1 can each whole kernel corn, peas
1 can chicken soup
1 lb. longhorn cheese, grated
Bread crumbs

Cook . . . . veal and pork in saucepan with water to cover until tender.
Drain . . . . . . reserving broth and cut meat into bite-sized pieces.
Cook . . . . noodles in broth until tender.
Add . . . . next 6 ingredients, meat and half the cheese, mixing well.
Spoon . . . . . . into baking dish.
Top . . . . with remaining cheese.
Sprinkle . . . . bread crumbs generously over top.
Bake . . . . at 350 degrees for 40 minutes.
Yields . . . . . . 15 servings.

Lois Scott
Xi Zeta Iota, Rocky River, Ohio

PARTY VEAL

8 lb. veal, cut into 1-in. pieces
1/2 c. oil
3/4 c. butter
Salt and pepper to taste
6 cans cream of mushroom soup
6 c. sliced onions
1/2 tsp. seasoned salt
1/4 tsp. Tabasco sauce
1/2 c. Sherry
2 c. sour cream

Brown . . . . . . veal in oil and 1/4 cup butter in skillet.
Remove . . . . to large roasting pan.
Add . . . . salt, pepper and soup.
Saute . . . . . . onions in 1/2 cup butter and pan drippings in skillet.
Pour . . . . over veal mixture.
Add . . . . seasoned salt, Tabasco sauce and 1/2 cup water to skillet.
Bring . . . . . . to a boil.
Pour . . . . over onions.
Bake . . . . covered, at 375 degrees for 45 minutes.
Add . . . . Sherry.
Bake . . . . uncovered, for 35 minutes.
Add . . . . sour cream, stirring gently.
Bake . . . . for 10 minutes longer.
Serve . . . . . . over rice.
Yields . . . . . . 24 servings.

Marilyn Fuher
Xi Alpha Iota, Pagosa Springs, Colorado

VEAL CASSEROLE

1 lb. thinly sliced veal cutlets
Flour
Salt and pepper to taste
3 tbsp. oil
1 c. rice, washed
2 beef bouillon cubes

Coat . . . . veal with flour seasoned with salt and pepper.
Brown . . . . . . in oil in skillet.
Layer . . . . . . veal and rice in 9-inch casserole.
Pour . . . . bouillon cubes dissolved in 2 1/3 cups boiling water over rice.
Bake . . . . covered, at 350 degrees for 50 to 60 minutes or until tender.

Linda Stewart
Xi Beta Psi, St. Louis, Missouri

Ground Beef

POT ROAST MEAT LOAF

1 lb. ground round
2/3 c. evaporated milk
1/3 c. oats
2 tsp. Worcestershire sauce
1/4 c. catsup
Salt
Pepper
3 potatoes, sliced 1/4-in. thick
3 onions, sliced 1/4-in. thick
3 carrots, quartered lengthwise
1 can golden mushroom soup

Combine .... first 5 ingredients, 1 teaspoon salt and 1/4 teaspoon pepper in bowl, mixing well.
Shape ...... into loaf in large casserole.
Arrange ..... vegetables around loaf.
Sprinkle .... generously with salt and pepper.
Pour .... soup over all.
Garnish ..... with parsley flakes.
Bake .... covered, at 375 degrees for 1 hour.

Sandy Johnson
Sigma Tau, Loomis, California

INDIVIDUAL MEAT LOAVES-FOR-A-CROWD

5 lb. each ground beef, ham, pork
2 c. cracker crumbs
1/2 tsp. pepper
9 eggs
Tomato soup
1/2 c. mustard
1/2 c. vinegar
1/2 c. sugar
1/2 c. butter, melted

Combine .... beef, ham, pork, crumbs and pepper in large bowl, mixing well.
Add .... 6 eggs and 4 cans tomato soup, mixing well.
Shape ...... into 2 x 4-inch loaves.
Place .... in large baking pans.
Bake .... at 350 degrees for 1 hour.
Mix .... mustard, vinegar, sugar and butter with 1/2 cup tomato soup and remaining 3 eggs.
Cook .... over low heat until custard coats spoon.

Serve .... over meat loaves.
Yields ...... 50 servings.

Hazel Fern Burns
Laureate Rho, Lamar, Colorado

BURRITO CASSEROLE

1 to 1 1/2 lb. ground beef
1 lg. onion, chopped
3 cloves of garlic, chopped
2 beef bouillon cubes
1 can chicken with rice soup
1 can enchilada sauce
1 can Ro-Tel
1 can chili beans
Flour tortillas
1 8-oz. carton sour cream
1 1/2 c. grated cheese

Brown ...... ground beef with onion and garlic in skillet, stirring until crumbly; drain.
Add .... next 5 ingredients, mixing well.
Simmer ..... for 10 minutes.
Layer ...... half the ground beef mixture, tortillas, sour cream and cheese in 9 x 13-inch baking dish.
Repeat ..... layers with remaining ingredients.
Bake .... at 375 degrees for 15 minutes.

Patsy Green
Xi Rho Kappa, Marshall, Texas

CREAMED TACOS

1 lb. Velveeta cheese, cubed
1 onion, chopped
1 can whole tomatoes
2 cans green chilies, chopped
1 sm. can evaporated milk
1 lb. hamburger
1 doz. corn tortillas

Combine .... first 5 ingredients in saucepan, mixing well.
Cook .... over low heat, until cheese is melted.
Brown ...... hamburger in skillet, stirring until crumbly; drain.
Soften ...... tortillas in hot oil in skillet.
Spoon ...... hamburger onto tortillas, rolling to enclose filling.
Arrange ..... seam side down in 9 x 11-inch baking pan.

Pour .... cheese sauce over tortillas.
Bake .... at 350 degrees for 25 to 30 minutes or until bubbly.
Serve .... with Spanish rice.
Yields ...... 6-8 servings.

Shirley Fitch
Xi Upsilon, Flagstaff, Arizona

FIESTA CASSEROLE

1 med. onion, chopped
1 tbsp. shortening
1 lb. hamburger
1 can whole kernel corn
1 can tamales, cut into bite-sized pieces
1 can garbanzo beans
1/2 can pitted ripe olives
1 can chili with beans
1/2 c. grated cheese

Saute ...... onion in shortening in skillet until tender.
Add .... hamburger.
Cook .... until brown, stirring until crumbly.
Drain ...... corn, reserving liquid.
Add .... corn with next 4 ingredients to hamburger, mixing well.
Place .... in 2-quart casserole.
Bake .... at 350 degrees for 45 minutes, adding reserved corn liquid if necessary.
Sprinkle .... with cheese.
Bake .... for 15 minutes longer.
Yields ...... 6 servings.

Becky Dickerson
Beta Kappa, Laurel, Montana

MEATBALL CHILI

1 lb. black-eyed peas
2 1/4 tsp. salt
2 to 2 1/2 lb. ground beef
1/2 c. crushed corn chips
1 med. onion, chopped
1 egg
1 15-oz. can tomato sauce
1 16-oz. can tomatoes
1 to 2 tbsp. chili powder
1/2 tsp. basil
1 clove of garlic, crushed
2 med. green peppers, coarsely chopped
2 tbsp. flour
2 tbsp. shortening

Combine .... black-eyed peas with 6 cups water and 1 teaspoon salt in large saucepan.
Boil .... for 2 minutes; remove from heat.
Let .... stand, covered, for 1 hour.
Cook .... covered, for 1 hour.
Combine .... ground beef with next 3 ingredients, 1 teaspoon salt and 1/2 cup tomato sauce in bowl, mixing well.
Shape ...... into balls.
Chill .... for 30 minutes or longer.
Combine .... remaining tomato sauce with tomatoes, 1/2 cup water, 1/4 teaspoon salt and next 3 ingredients in large saucepan.
Simmer ..... for 30 minutes, stirring occasionally.
Drain ...... black-eyed peas reserving liquid.
Stir .... peas and green pepper with 1 1/2 cups reserved liquid into tomato mixture.
Coat .... meatballs with flour.
Brown ..... in shortening in skillet.
Add .... to tomato mixture.
Cook .... tightly covered, for 30 minutes or until black-eyed peas are tender.
Serve .... with corn chips.
Yields ...... 8 servings.

Photograph for this recipe on cover.

MEXICAN CASSEROLE

1 lb. ground beef
1 15-oz. can hot chili with beans
8 oz. mozzarella cheese, shredded
1 6-oz. can chili without beans
1 pkg. tortilla chips, crushed

Brown ...... ground beef in skillet, stirring until crumbly.
Layer ...... ground beef, chili with beans, half the cheese and chili without beans in casserole.
Top .... with remaining cheese and tortilla chips.
Bake .... at 375 degrees for 30 minutes or until heated through.

Sherry McKie
Zeta Iota, Creston, Iowa

BAKED NACHOS

1/2 lb. ground beef
1/2 lb. beef chorizo sausage, sliced
1 onion, chopped
1 4-oz. can green chilies, chopped
1 30-oz. can refried beans
3 c. shredded cheese
1 10-oz. bottle of taco sauce

Brown . . . . . . ground beef and chorizo sausage with onion in skillet, stirring until ground beef is crumbly; drain.

Layer . . . . . . sausage mixture, chilies, beans, cheese and taco sauce in casserole.

Bake . . . . at 350 degrees for 20 to 30 minutes or until heated through.

Serve . . . . . . with sour cream and nacho chips.

Vicki Pope
Gamma Omega, Kingman, Arizona

BEEF AND TATER PIE

1 lb. lean ground beef
1 unbaked deep-dish pie shell
1/2 can cream of mushroom soup
Frozen French-fried potatoes
1/2 c. shredded cheese

Press . . . . half the ground beef in bottom of pie shell.

Layer . . . . . . soup, remaining ground beef and potatoes over top.

Bake . . . . at 350 degrees for 1 hour.

Top . . . . with cheese.

Bake . . . . for several minutes longer or until cheese melts.

Pam Kellett
Delta Tau, Thomaston, Georgia

COUNTRY PIE

1 lb. hamburger
1/2 c. bread crumbs
1/8 tsp. pepper
1 1/2 tsp. salt
2 1/2 c. tomato sauce
1 1/3 c. rice
1 c. grated cheese

Combine . . . . first 3 ingredients with 1 teaspoon salt and 1 cup tomato sauce in bowl, mixing well.

Press . . . . . . into 9-inch pie plate.

Combine . . . . rice, cheese, 1/2 teaspoon salt, 1 cup water and remaining 1 1/2 cups tomato sauce in bowl, mixing well.

Pour . . . . into prepared pie plate.

Bake . . . . covered, at 350 degrees for 25 minutes.

Sprinkle . . . . additional cheese over top.

Bake . . . . uncovered, for 10 to 15 minutes longer or until cheese melts.

Yields . . . . . . 4 servings.

Betty Vandament
Preceptor Delta Gamma, Lawrenceville, Illinois

HOT TAMALE PIE CASSEROLE

1 1/2 lb. ground beef
2 lg. onions, chopped
1 16-oz. can tomatoes
3 tbsp. chili powder
Salt
Pepper to taste
3/4 c. cornmeal

Brown . . . . . . ground beef in skillet, stirring until crumbly; drain.

Add . . . . next 3 ingredients with salt and pepper to taste, mixing well.

Cook . . . . until thick.

Mix . . . . cornmeal with enough cold water in bowl to make paste.

Bring . . . . 1 1/2 cups water to a boil in saucepan.

Spoon . . . . . . cornmeal mixture and 1 teaspoon salt into boiling water, stirring constantly.

Cook . . . . until thick.

Pour . . . . into 2-quart casserole.

Top . . . . with ground beef mixture.

Bake . . . . at 375 degrees for 20 minutes.

Garnish . . . . . with ripe olives.

Yields . . . . . . 6-8 servings.

Norma L. Geirk
Preceptor Theta Delta, Vista, California

CHEESY PIZZA CASSEROLE

2 to 3 lb. ground beef
1 sm. package frozen onions, thawed
Salt and pepper to taste
2 med. cans sliced mushrooms, drained
2 jars pizza sauce

3 c. shredded mozzarella cheese
1 box croutons
Parmesan cheese

Brown . . . . . . ground beef with onions, salt and pepper in skillet, stirring until crumbly; drain.
Combine . . . . with mushrooms, pizza sauce, half the mozzarella cheese, half the croutons and a small amount of Parmesan cheese in casserole, mixing well.
Top . . . . with remaining mozzarella cheese and croutons.
Sprinkle . . . . Parmesan cheese over top.
Bake . . . . at 400 degrees for 10 minutes or until cheese is melted.
Yields . . . . . . 8-10 servings.

Karey A. Crofford
Gamma Theta, Falls City, Nebraska

POOR MAN'S TURKEY

1 1/2 to 2 lb. ground beef
14 slices day-old bread, cubed
1 lg. onion, chopped
1/4 lb. margarine, melted
Salt and pepper to taste
2 cans each cream of chicken, cream of celery soup
Sage, oregano to taste

Press . . . . ground beef over bottom of greased 9 x 13-inch baking pan.
Combine . . . . bread, onion, margarine, salt and pepper in bowl, mixing well.
Spoon . . . . . . over ground beef.
Mix . . . . soups in bowl.
Spread . . . . . over bread mixture.
Sprinkle . . . . lightly with sage and oregano.
Bake . . . . at 350 degrees for 1 to 1 1/2 hours or until brown.
Yields . . . . . . 8-10 servings.

Deborah E. Fletcher
Delta Psi, Clare, Michigan

HAMBURGER STROGANOFF

1 1/2 lb. ground chuck
1 lg. onion, chopped
1 clove of garlic, chopped
Salt and pepper to taste
1 can golden mushroom soup

1 1/2 tsp. paprika
1 beef bouillon cube
1/4 c. dry wine
1/2 c. sour cream
1 can French-fried onions

Brown . . . . . . ground chuck lightly in skillet, stirring until crumbly.
Add . . . . onion, garlic, salt and pepper.
Cook . . . . until onion is tender, stirring frequently.
Stir . . . . in soup, paprika and bouillon.
Simmer . . . . . for 10 minutes.
Add . . . . wine.
Bring . . . . to a simmer; remove from heat.
Stir . . . . in sour cream.
Top . . . . with French-fried onions.
Serve . . . . over noodles.
Yields . . . . . . 8 servings.

Marlene Niesinger
Preceptor Mu, Neosho, Missouri

CAVATINI

1 lb. ground beef
1 clove of garlic, chopped
1 each med. onion, green pepper, chopped
1/2 lb. pepperoni, thinly sliced
1 sm. can mushrooms, drained
1   32-oz. jar spaghetti sauce
1/4 lb. curly noodles, cooked, drained
1/4 lb. shell macaroni, cooked, drained
1/2 lb. mozzarella cheese, grated

Brown . . . . . . ground beef in skillet, stirring until crumbly.
Add . . . . garlic, onion and green pepper.
Cook . . . . until tender, stirring frequently; drain.
Stir . . . . in pepperoni, mushrooms and spaghetti sauce.
Combine . . . . noodles and macaroni.
Layer . . . . . . noodle mixture, cheese and ground beef mixture alternately in greased 9 x 13-inch baking dish.
Bake . . . . at 375 degrees for 35 to 40 minutes or until bubbly.
Let . . . . stand for 10 minutes before serving.
Yields . . . . . . 8-10 servings.

Evelyn Configliacco
Xi Rho, Lead, South Dakota

GOULASH AND TATER TOTS

1 lb. hamburger
1 med. onion, chopped
1 can tomato soup
1/2 to 1 c. catsup
1 c. elbow macaroni, cooked
1 to 2 tbsp. Worcestershire sauce
Salt and pepper to taste
Tater Tots

Brown ...... hamburger with onion in skillet, stirring until crumbly.
Add .... next 6 ingredients, mixing well.
Spoon ...... into 2-quart casserole.
Top .... with Tater Tots.
Bake .... at 350 degrees until bubbly, adding water if necessary.

Sue Moss
Zeta Beta, Jacksonville, Illinois

MACARONI-BEEF CASSEROLE

1 lb. lean ground beef
Chopped onion
1 c. coarsely chopped green pepper
1 clove of garlic, minced
1/4 c. oil
1 16-oz. can tomatoes, drained, chopped
1 6-oz. can tomato paste
1/2 tsp. oregano
Dash of pepper
Salt to taste
1 c. elbow macaroni, cooked
1 can whole kernel corn
1 c. shredded mozzarella cheese

Brown ...... ground beef with onion, green pepper and garlic in oil in skillet, stirring until crumbly; remove from heat.
Stir .... in next 7 ingredients.
Spoon ...... into 3-quart casserole.
Sprinkle .... cheese over top.
Bake .... at 350 degrees for 35 to 45 minutes or until bubbly.
Yields ...... 6-8 servings.

Flo Helmer
Beta Nu, Encampment, Wyoming

CHUCK WAGON STEW

1 lb. ground beef
1/4 c. chopped onion

1 tsp. salt
1/8 tsp. pepper
2 tbsp. butter
1 c. chopped celery
2 c. cubed cheese
2 c. egg noodles
1 16-oz. can stewed tomatoes

Brown ...... ground beef with onion, salt and pepper in butter in skillet, stirring until crumbly.
Place .... in 2-quart casserole.
Combine .... remaining ingredients in bowl, mixing well.
Spoon ...... over ground beef mixture.
Pour .... 1/2 cup water over top.
Bake .... covered, at 400 degrees for 45 minutes. Do not peek.
Yields ...... 6 servings.

Barb Solheim
Xi Gamma Rho, Clinton, Iowa

MANICOTTI STUFFED WITH MEAT

1 tbsp. oil
2 8-oz. cans tomato sauce
1 6-oz. can tomato paste
1 tsp. sugar
1 1/2 tsp. basil
3 tbsp. each finely chopped green pepper, onion
1 1/2 tsp. salt
1/2 tsp. pepper
1/2 c. Parmesan cheese
3/4 c. each ground beef, sausage
3 tbsp. flour
1/8 tsp. cayenne pepper
1/2 tsp. paprika
3 tbsp. butter, melted
Milk
2 eggs, well beaten
1/2 tsp. each garlic powder, oregano
1/4 c. grated sharp Cheddar cheese
1/4 c. chopped green pepper
1 med. onion, chopped
8 manicotti shells, cooked
1 c. shredded mozzarella cheese

Combine .... first 7 ingredients, 1 teaspoon salt, 1/4 teaspoon pepper and 1/4 cup Parmesan cheese in large saucepan, mixing well.
Simmer ..... until onion is tender.

Brown . . . . . . ground beef and sausage in skillet, stirring until crumbly; drain.

Blend . . . . . . flour, cayenne pepper, paprika and remaining 1/2 teaspoon salt with butter in saucepan.

Stir . . . . in 1 cup milk gradually.

Cook . . . . over low heat until thick, stirring constantly.

Spread . . . . . 1/2 cup white sauce in well-greased 9 x 13-inch baking dish.

Stir . . . . a small amount of remaining hot white sauce into eggs; stir eggs into white sauce.

Add . . . . next 5 ingredients, ground beef mixture, 2 tablespoons milk, remaining 1/4 cup Parmesan cheese and 1/4 teaspoon pepper, mixing well.

Spoon . . . . . . into manicotti shells.

Place . . . . in prepared baking dish.

Pour . . . . prepared tomato sauce over shells.

Top . . . . with mozzarella cheese and additional Parmesan cheese.

Bake . . . . at 350 degrees for 40 to 45 minutes or until bubbly.

Yields . . . . . . 8-10 servings.

Pamela Welter
Theta Rho, New Hampton, Iowa

SO-SIMPLE LASAGNA

1 1/2 lb. ground beef
1 16-oz. can whole tomatoes
2 12-oz. cans V-8 juice
2 env. spaghetti sauce mix
1 lb. lasagna noodles
1 16-oz. carton cottage cheese
8 oz. mozzarella cheese, shredded
1/4 c. Parmesan cheese

Brown . . . . . . ground beef in skillet, stirring until crumbly.

Stir . . . . in next 3 ingredients.

Layer . . . . . . ground beef mixture, uncooked noodles, cottage cheese, mozzarella cheese and Parmesan cheese in greased 9 x 13-inch baking dish.

Chill . . . . covered, for several hours or overnight.

Bake . . . . covered, at 350 degrees for 45 minutes.

Bake . . . . uncovered, for 15 minutes longer.

Let . . . . stand for 15 minutes before cutting.

Yields . . . . . . 6-8 servings.

Janice Ryan
Xi Beta Chi, Grand Island, Nebraska

SPAGHETTI CASSEROLE

1 lb. ground beef
1 onion, chopped
1/2 green pepper, chopped
1 can each tomato, mushroom soup
1/2 lb. spaghetti, cooked, drained
1 1/2 c. grated cheese
Salt and pepper to taste

Brown . . . . . . ground beef with onion and green pepper in skillet, stirring until crumbly.

Stir . . . . in soups and 1 cup water.

Simmer . . . . . for several minutes.

Add . . . . spaghetti, 1 cup cheese, salt and pepper, mixing well.

Spoon . . . . . . into 2 1/2-quart casserole.

Sprinkle . . . . with remaining 1/2 cup cheese.

Bake . . . . in moderate oven until bubbly and cheese is melted.

Yields . . . . . . 6 servings.

Judy Kirkley
Xi Alpha Omega, Crossett, Arkansas

SPANISH RICE

4 slices bacon, chopped
1 lb. ground beef
1 onion, chopped
1 green pepper, diced
1 1/4 tsp. salt
1/2 tsp. paprika
1 can tomatoes
3/4 c. rice, cooked

Brown . . . . . . bacon and ground beef with onion and green pepper in skillet, stirring until crumbly; drain.

Add . . . . remaining 4 ingredients, mixing well.

Spoon . . . . . . into 1-quart casserole.

Bake . . . . at 350 degrees for 30 minutes.

Yields . . . . . . 4 servings.

B. A. DeLucry
Delta Mu, Toronto, Ontario, Canada

LAYERED CASSEROLE ITALIANO

4 to 5 c. sliced zucchini
1 c. minced onion
1 sm. clove of garlic, crushed
2 tbsp. butter
1 lb. ground beef
1 c. minute rice
1 tsp. basil
1 16-oz. carton cream-style cottage
  cheese
1 can tomato soup
1 c. shredded sharp American cheese

Cook .... zucchini in a small amount of salted water in saucepan until tender; drain.
Saute ...... onion and garlic in butter in skillet.
Add .... ground beef.
Cook .... until light brown, stirring until crumbly.
Stir .... in rice and basil.
Arrange ..... half the zucchini in 2 1/2-quart casserole.
Layer ...... ground beef mixture, cottage cheese and remaining zucchini over top.
Pour .... soup mixed with 2/3 cup water over top.
Sprinkle .... cheese over all.
Bake .... at 350 degrees for 35 to 40 minutes or until light brown.
Yields ...... 6-8 servings.

Photograph for this recipe on page 43.

TEXAS HASH

3 lg. onions, sliced
1 lg. green pepper, finely chopped
3 tbsp. oil
1 lb. ground beef
1 16-oz. can tomatoes, mashed
1/2 c. rice
1 tsp. chili powder
2 tsp. salt
1/8 tsp. pepper

Saute ...... onions and green pepper in oil in skillet until onions are golden.
Brown ...... ground beef with sauteed vegetables, stirring until crumbly.
Stir .... in remaining ingredients.
Pour .... into greased 2-quart baking dish.

Bake .... covered, at 350 degrees for 45 minutes.
Bake .... uncovered, for 15 minutes longer.
Yields ...... 6 servings.

Irene Connolly
Xi Alpha Lambda, Norfolk, Virginia

WILD RICE CASSEROLE

1 c. wild rice
1 lb. ground beef
Chopped onion to taste
1 can mushrooms, drained
1 can mushroom soup
1 can bean sprouts, drained
Salt and pepper to taste
Chopped celery, green pepper (opt.)

Wash .... rice in cold water.
Cook .... covered, in 3 cups boiling water in saucepan for 5 minutes; remove from heat.
Let .... stand for 1 hour; drain and rinse.
Brown ...... ground beef with onion and mushrooms in skillet, stirring until crumbly.
Add .... rice, 1/2 cup water and remaining ingredients, mixing well.
Spoon ...... into 1 1/2-quart casserole.
Bake .... at 350 degrees for 1 1/2 hours.
Yields ...... 12-15 servings.

Doris H. Cosco
Xi Delta Mu, Sioux Lookout, Ontario, Canada

QUICK HAMBURGER CASSEROLE

1 lb. hamburger
2 tbsp. minced onion
1 can green beans, drained
1 can cream of mushroom soup
1 sm. package Tater Tots

Brown ...... hamburger with onion in skillet, stirring until crumbly.
Layer ...... hamburger mixture, green beans, soup and Tater Tots in 2-quart casserole.
Bake .... at 350 degrees for 40 minutes.
Yields ...... 4 servings.

Cheryl Hamilton
Xi Epsilon Iota, Manchester, Michigan

BEEF AND BARLEY SUPREME

2 lb. hamburger
3/4 c. barley, cooked
1 1/2 green peppers, chopped
2 c. chopped celery
2 cans tomato soup
1 c. canned mushrooms with liquid
2 tsp. salt
1 sm. package frozen peas and corn

Brown . . . . . . hamburger in skillet, stirring until crumbly.
Add . . . . remaining ingredients, mixing well.
Spoon . . . . . . into 9 x 13-inch baking dish.
Bake . . . . at 325 degrees for 2 hours, adding water if necessary.
Pour . . . . off excess drippings before serving.
Yields . . . . . . 16 servings.

Annette Cloward
Xi Gamma Eta, Seattle, Washington

HUNGRY JACK BEEF CASSEROLE

1 lb. ground beef
1 31-oz. can pork and beans
3/4 c. barbecue sauce
2 tbsp. brown sugar
1 tbsp. instant minced onion
1 tsp. salt
1 can refrigerator biscuits, cut
*   into halves*
1 c. shredded Cheddar cheese

Brown . . . . . . ground beef in skillet, stirring until crumbly; drain.
Add . . . . next 5 ingredients, mixing well.
Cook . . . . until bubbly.
Pour . . . . into 2-quart casserole.
Arrange . . . . . biscuits cut side down around edge of casserole.
Sprinkle . . . . cheese over top.
Bake . . . . at 375 degrees for 30 minutes or until golden brown.
Yields . . . . . . 4 servings.

Teri L. Laird
Upsilon, Powell, Wyoming

CAULIFLOWER-BEEF CASSEROLE

1 med. head cauliflower, separated
1 1/2 lb. ground beef
1 sm. onion, chopped
1/2 tsp. salt
1/2 tsp. Tabasco sauce
1 tbsp. flour
1 c. milk
1 tbsp. oil
2 c. grated cheese
1 c. seasoned bread cubes

Cook . . . . cauliflower in salted water in saucepan until tender-crisp; drain.
Saute . . . . . . ground beef with onion, salt and 1/4 teaspoon Tabasco sauce, stirring until crumbly; set aside.
Blend . . . . . . flour, milk, oil and 1/4 teaspoon Tabasco in small saucepan.
Cook . . . . over low heat until thickened, stirring constantly.
Add . . . . cheese.
Cook . . . . until cheese melts, stirring constantly.
Layer . . . . . . ground beef mixture, bread cubes, cauliflower and cheese sauce in 2-quart casserole.
Bake . . . . at 375 degrees for 1/2 hour or until hot and bubbly.
Yields . . . . . . 6 servings.

Photograph for this recipe below.

BEAN SPROUT CASSEROLE

1 lb. hamburger
1 med. onion, chopped
1 can each cream of chicken, cream of
*   mushroom soup*
1 c. sliced celery
3/4 c. minute rice
1 can bean sprouts
6 tbsp. soy sauce

Brown . . . . . . hamburger with onion in skillet, stirring until crumbly.
Add . . . . remaining ingredients, mixing well.
Spoon . . . . . . into greased 2 1/2-quart casserole.
Bake . . . . at 350 degrees for 1 1/2 hours.
Serve . . . . . . with chow mein noodles.
Yields . . . . . . 6 servings.

Debbie Alber
Lambda Nu, Manchester, Michigan

ORIENTAL BEEF

1 lb. ground beef
3 tbsp. soy sauce
1 sm. head cabbage, sliced
3 green onions, chopped
1 green pepper, chopped
2 c. sliced celery
1 can bean sprouts
1 can mushrooms
1 can cream of celery soup
1/2 c. cream
1/2 c. bread crumbs
2 tbsp. butter

Brown . . . . . . ground beef in skillet, stirring until crumbly; drain.
Add . . . . soy sauce, mixing well.
Layer . . . . . . cabbage, green onions, green pepper, celery, bean sprouts, mushrooms and ground beef in large greased casserole.
Cook . . . . soup and cream in saucepan until blended.
Pour . . . . over casserole.
Sprinkle . . . . with bread crumbs.
Dot . . . . with butter.
Bake . . . . at 375 degrees for 1 1/2 hours.

Sharry Yaeck
Xi Eta, Red Deer, Alberta, Canada

BROCCOLI CASSEROLE

1/2 lb. ground beef
3 c. cooked broccoli
1/2 c. evaporated milk
1 egg, slightly beaten
1 can cream of chicken soup
1 c. grated Cheddar cheese
1 c. bread stuffing mix
3 tbsp. butter, melted

Brown . . . . . . ground beef in skillet; stirring until crumbly; drain.
Add . . . . next 4 ingredients, mixing well.
Spoon . . . . . . into buttered casserole.
Combine . . . . cheese, stuffing mix and butter in bowl, mixing well.
Sprinkle . . . . over ground beef mixture.
Bake . . . . at 350 degrees for 25 minutes.
May . . . . substitute asparagus, cauliflower, eggplant or zucchini for broccoli.

Gladys Kozisek
Preceptor Alpha, Lincoln, Nebraska

CABBAGE CASSEROLE

1 med. head cabbage, chopped
1 lb. ground beef
2 stalks celery, chopped
1 med. onion, chopped
5 cloves of garlic, chopped
1 can cream of mushroom soup
3/4 c. Parmesan cheese
1/2 c. Italian bread crumbs
Salt and pepper to taste

Cook . . . . cabbage in boiling water in saucepan until tender; drain.
Brown . . . . . . ground beef in large skillet, stirring until crumbly.
Add . . . . celery, onion and garlic.
Saute . . . . . . until tender.
Add . . . . soup and 1/2 soup can water, mixing well.
Simmer . . . . . for several minutes.
Stir . . . . in cabbage, cheese, bread crumbs, salt and pepper.
Spoon . . . . . . into 8 x 11-inch baking dish.
Top . . . . with additional cheese and bread crumbs.
Bake . . . . at 400 degrees until brown.

Maria Lambert
Iota Delta, La Place, Louisiana

MOCK CABBAGE ROLLS

1 sm. head cabbage, coarsely chopped
1 lb. ground beef
1/2 c. chopped onion
1/2 c. rice
1/2 tsp. salt
1/4 tsp. pepper
1 can tomato soup
1/2 c. grated cheese

Place . . . . cabbage over bottom of greased 9 x 13-inch baking dish.
Brown . . . . . . ground beef with onion in skillet, stirring until crumbly.
Stir . . . . in rice, salt and pepper.
Spoon . . . . . . over cabbage.
Bring . . . . soup blended with 1 1/2 cups water to a boil in saucepan.
Pour . . . . over ground beef mixture.
Top . . . . with cheese.
Bake . . . . covered, at 350 degrees for 1 1/2 hours.
Stir . . . . lightly with fork before serving.
Yields . . . . . . 6 servings.

Lorraine Danney
Preceptor Laureate Gamma, Buffalo, New York

EGGPLANT CASSEROLE

1 lb. ground beef
2 med. onions, finely chopped
1/2 c. olive oil
1/2 c. tomato paste
2 tbsp. minced parsley
1/4 lb. butter
Salt and pepper to taste
2 med. eggplant, peeled, cut lengthwise 1/4 in. thick
Flour
1/2 c. bread crumbs
2 eggs, well beaten
1/2 c. grated cheese

Brown . . . . . . ground beef with onions in a small amount of olive oil in skillet, stirring until crumbly.
Add . . . . next 5 ingredients and 1 cup water, mixing well.
Simmer . . . . . for 1 hour or until thick.
Sprinkle . . . . eggplant with flour.
Brown . . . . . . in olive oil in skillet.
Stir . . . . 2 tablespoons bread crumbs into ground beef mixture.

Sprinkle . . . . half the remaining bread crumbs over buttered 9 x 13-inch baking dish.
Layer . . . . . . eggplant and ground beef mixture alternately in prepared baking dish.
Pour . . . . eggs evenly over top.
Top . . . . with cheese and remaining bread crumbs.
Bake . . . . in moderate oven for 30 minutes or until golden brown.

Georgia Martino
Rho Eta, Oroville, California

BUSY DAY CASSEROLE

Sliced potatoes
Thinly sliced carrots
Rice
1 lb. ground beef
Thinly sliced onions
4 c. canned tomatoes
1 tbsp. sugar
Salt and pepper to taste

Layer . . . . . . first 6 ingredients in 2-quart baking dish in order given.
Sprinkle . . . . with sugar, salt and pepper.
Bake . . . . covered, for 2 hours or until vegetables are tender.

Jean White
Preceptor Zeta, Brewer, Maine

MEATBALL CASSEROLE

1 lb. ground beef
2 c. grated potatoes
2 c. grated carrots
1 sm. onion, chopped
Salt and pepper to taste
1 can cream of mushroom soup
3/4 c. milk

Combine . . . . first 6 ingredients in bowl, mixing well.
Shape . . . . . . into patties.
Brown . . . . . . on both sides in skillet.
Place . . . . in casserole.
Blend . . . . . . soup and milk in bowl.
Pour . . . . over patties.
Bake . . . . at 350 degrees for 1 to 1 1/2 hours.

Lynnette J. Koens
Xi Beta Chi, Medford, Oregon

BEEF AND POTATO CASSEROLE

1 c. thinly sliced carrots
2 med. potatoes, thinly sliced
1 med. onion, sliced
2 tbsp. chopped green chilies
1 tsp. salt
1/4 tsp. pepper
1 can cream of mushroom soup
1 lb. ground beef
1/4 c. quick oats
1 tsp. prepared mustard

Combine .... first 4 ingredients, 3/4 teaspoon salt, 1/8 teaspoon pepper and 1/3 of the soup in bowl, mixing well.
Place .... in 6 x 10-inch baking dish.
Combine .... 1/3 of the soup, remaining salt and pepper, ground beef and oats in bowl, mixing well.
Spread ..... over vegetables.
Bake .... covered, at 350 degrees for 1 1/4 hours.
Mix .... remaining soup with mustard in bowl.
Spread ..... over ground beef.
Bake .... for 15 minutes longer.
Yields ...... 4 servings.

Christine Walter
Lambda Upsilon, Burlington, Iowa

ZUCCHINI-TOMATO BAKE

1 1/2 c. chopped onion
1 c. coarsely chopped celery
1 lb. ground beef
3 to 4 c. sliced zucchini
1 tbsp. butter
1 1/2 c. tomato sauce
1 1/2 tsp. garlic salt
2 tsp. oregano
1/2 c. Parmesan cheese

Saute ...... onion and celery in skillet until tender-crisp; remove.
Brown ...... ground beef in skillet, stirring until crumbly; remove.
Brown ...... zucchini lightly in butter in skillet.
Spoon ...... vegetables and ground beef into 9 x 13-inch casserole, mixing lightly.
Pour .... tomato sauce over all.

Sprinkle .... with garlic salt and oregano.
Top .... with Parmesan cheese.
Yields ...... 6 servings.

Lois Frazer
Xi Eta, Hanover, New Hampshire

SPINACH HOT DISH

1 1/2 lb. hamburger
1 sm. onion, chopped
2 pkg. frozen spinach, cooked
1/2 tsp. garlic powder
1/4 tsp. oregano
6 eggs
1/4 c. milk

Brown ...... hamburger with onion in skillet, stirring until crumbly.
Mix .... in spinach and seasonings.
Beat .... eggs and milk together in bowl until light.
Add .... to spinach mixture, mixing well.
Cook .... over low heat until eggs are cooked through, stirring occasionally.
Serve .... with Italian bread.
Yields ...... 5-6 servings.

Lucylle Doerr
Lodgepole Chapter, Hettinger, North Dakota

SPINACH AND MEAT PIE

3/4 lb. ground beef
1 tsp. salt
1/8 tsp. pepper
1 c. sliced onion
1 pkg. frozen spinach, cooked, drained
1/2 tsp. Worcestershire sauce
3 eggs, beaten
1 c. cream sauce

Brown ...... ground beef with salt and pepper in skillet, stirring until crumbly.
Add .... onion.
Cook .... until tender, stirring frequently.
Stir .... in remaining ingredients.
Spread ..... in pie plate.
Bake .... at 350 degrees for 30 minutes or until lightly browned.
Yields ...... 6 servings.

Carol D. Drumluk
Gamma Iota, Rome, New York

Pork

SCALLOPED BACON AND EGG CASSEROLE

1/4 c. chopped onion
2 tbsp. butter
2 tbsp. flour
1 1/2 c. milk
1 c. shredded sharp cheese
6 hard-boiled eggs, sliced
1 1/2 c. crushed potato chips
10 to 12 slices crisp-cooked bacon, crumbled

Saute ...... onion in butter in skillet until tender.
Mix .... in flour then milk.
Cook .... until thick, stirring constantly.
Stir .... in cheese.
Cook .... until cheese is melted, stirring constantly.
Layer ...... half the eggs, cheese mixture, potato chips and bacon in 1 1/2-quart casserole.
Repeat ..... layers with remaining ingredients.
Bake .... at 350 degrees for 15 to 20 minutes or until heated through.

Florence Marcucci
Xi Theta Phi, Ballwin, Missouri

HAM AND EGGS CASSEROLE

1 8-oz. package refrigerator crescent rolls, separated
1 c. chopped ham
4 eggs
1/2 c. milk
1 tsp. salt
1/4 tsp. pepper
1 tbsp. chopped chives
1 c. grated Swiss cheese

Press .... sheets of crescent roll dough into bottom and 1/2 inch up sides of greased 9 x 13-inch baking pan.
Place .... ham over dough.
Beat .... next 4 ingredients together in bowl.
Pour .... over ham.
Top .... with chives and cheese.
Bake .... at 350 degrees for 25 to 30 minutes or until set.

Diane Garrison
Mu Mu, Edinboro, Pennsylvania

HAWAIIAN HAM

2 1/2 c. diced cooked ham
1 med. onion, sliced, separated into rings
1 sm. green pepper, cut into rings
1 c. drained pineapple chunks
1/2 c. raisins
2 tsp. dry mustard
1/4 tsp. salt
1/2 c. packed brown sugar
2 tbsp. cornstarch
1 c. pineapple syrup
1/3 c. vinegar
1 tsp. Worcestershire sauce
1 tbsp. soy sauce

Layer ...... first 5 ingredients in casserole.
Combine .... mustard, salt, brown sugar and cornstarch in saucepan, mixing well.
Stir .... in pineapple syrup and vinegar.
Bring ...... to a boil, stirring constantly.
Cook .... until clear, stirring constantly.
Blend ...... in remaining 2 ingredients.
Pour .... over casserole.
Bake .... at 350 degrees for 45 minutes to 1 hour or until bubbly.
Serve .... over rice.
Yields ...... 6 servings.

Fran Parks
Preceptor Beta Chi, St. Charles, Missouri

POTATO CHIP-HAM CASSEROLE

4 tbsp. butter, melted
4 tbsp. flour
2 1/4 c. milk
1 1/2 c. diced ham
Mushrooms (opt.)
2 c. slightly crushed potato chips

Blend ...... butter and flour in saucepan.
Add .... milk, mixing well.
Cook .... until thick and smooth, stirring constantly.
Add .... ham and mushrooms, mixing well.
Pour .... into greased 1 1/2-quart casserole.
Top .... with potato chips.
Bake .... at 350 degrees for 30 minutes.

Helen Zigich
Preceptor Epsilon, Duluth, Minnesota

HAM ITALIAN

1 4-oz. can sliced mushrooms, drained
1/2 c. each chopped green pepper, onion,
celery
1/2 c. margarine
1 to 2 c. diced cooked ham
1 8 1/4-oz. can green peas, drained
1 2-oz. jar chopped pimentos
1 8-oz. package flat egg noodles,
cooked, drained
3/4 c. cheese cubes
1 can mushroom soup
1/4 tsp. garlic salt
3/4 c. Parmesan cheese

Saute ...... first 4 ingredients in margarine
in skillet.
Add .... ham, peas, pimentos, noodles,
cheese cubes, soup and garlic
salt, mixing well.
Cook .... until heated through.
Spoon ...... into 3-quart casserole.
Sprinkle .... with Parmesan cheese.
Bake .... at 350 degrees for 10 to 15 min-
utes or until bubbly.
Yields ...... 6-8 servings.

Lucy Doty
Xi Gamma Alpha, Baton Rouge, Louisiana

CHEESY HAM AND VEGETABLE CASSEROLE

1/2 c. flour
1/4 tsp. salt
1/8 tsp. white pepper
1 tsp. dry mustard
1 tsp. Worcestershire sauce
3 c. milk
1/2 c. melted butter
1 sm. onion, grated
1 1/2 c. grated sharp cheese
2 pkg. frozen mixed vegetables,
cooked, drained
1 lb. cooked ham, cubed
2 c. soft bread crumbs

Combine .... first 5 ingredients with 1/3 cup
milk in bowl, mixing well.
Stir .... into 2 2/3 cups heated milk with
6 tablespoons butter in
saucepan.
Cook .... over low heat until thickened,
stirring constantly.

Add .... onion and cheese.
Cook .... until cheese is melted, stirring
constantly.
Stir .... in vegetables and ham.
Pour .... into 8 x 12-inch baking dish.
Toss .... bread crumbs with remaining 2
tablespoons butter in bowl.
Sprinkle .... over casserole.
Bake .... at 350 degrees until crumbs are
brown.

Vera Derrick Epperson
Preceptor Alpha Nu, El Paso, Texas

HAM AND ARTICHOKE CASSEROLE

12 thin slices boiled ham
2 16-oz. cans artichoke hearts, drained
4 tbsp. butter, melted
4 tbsp. flour
2 c. warm milk
2/3 c. shredded Swiss cheese
Parmesan cheese
Dash each of seasoned salt, cayenne
pepper
1/4 tsp. each nutmeg, paprika
Pinch of white pepper
4 tbsp. dry Sherry
Bread crumbs, buttered, toasted

Wrap .... 1 slice ham around each arti-
choke heart.
Arrange ..... in buttered casserole with sides
touching.
Blend ...... butter and flour in saucepan.
Stir .... in milk gradually.
Cook .... until thick and smooth, stirring
constantly.
Mix .... Swiss cheese with 2/3 cup Par-
mesan cheese in bowl.
Stir .... into sauce with seasonings.
Cook .... over low heat until cheese is
melted, stirring constantly; re-
move from heat.
Stir .... in Sherry.
Pour .... over ham-wrapped artichokes.
Mix .... bread crumbs with equal amount
Parmesan cheese.
Sprinkle .... over casserole.
Bake .... at 350 degrees for 25 to 30 min-
utes or until brown and bubbly.
Yields ...... 6 servings.

Margaret G. Hendricks
Xi Beta Tau, Little Rock, Arkansas

BROCCOLI AND HAM STRATA

12 slices white bread, trimmed
1 lb. shredded Cheddar cheese
1 lb. frozen chopped broccoli, thawed,
  drained
2 c. diced cooked ham
6 eggs
3 1/2 c. milk
1 tsp. dry mustard
1 tsp. Worcestershire sauce
2 tbsp. instant minced onion
1/2 tsp. garlic powder
1/8 tsp. cayenne pepper

Cut . . . . bread with 3-inch doughnut cutter; set rings aside.
Cut . . . . remaining bread into cubes.
Layer . . . . . . 3/4 of the cheese, bread cubes, broccoli, ham and bread rings in greased 9 x 13-inch baking dish.
Top . . . . with remaining cheese.
Beat . . . . remaining 7 ingredients together in bowl until well blended.
Pour . . . . evenly over casserole.
Chill . . . . covered, for 12 hours.
Bake . . . . uncovered, at 350 degrees for 1 hour or until center is set.
Let . . . . stand for 15 minutes before cutting.
Yields . . . . . . 12 servings.

Karen S. Fitch
Xi Xi Mu, Bakersfield, California

HAM-POTATO BAKE

1 1/2 c. cubed cooked ham
1 can cream of mushroom soup
1/4 c. milk
1 tbsp. instant minced onion
1/8 tsp. pepper
1 c. shredded sharp American cheese
4 c. sliced cooked potatoes
1 c. shredded carrots
3/4 c. soft bread crumbs
1 tbsp. butter, melted

Combine . . . . first 5 ingredients and 1/2 cup cheese in bowl, mixing well.
Layer . . . . . . half the potatoes, carrots and ham mixture in 2-quart casserole.
Repeat . . . . . layers with remaining ingredients.

Mix . . . . bread crumbs, remaining 1/2 cup cheese and butter in bowl.
Sprinkle . . . . over casserole.
Bake . . . . at 350 degrees for 45 minutes or until heated through.
Garnish . . . . . with sprigs of parsley.
Yields . . . . . . 4-6 servings.

Judy Davis
Alpha Beta, McComb, Mississippi

HAM AND SPINACH

1 pkg. frozen chopped spinach,
  cooked, drained
1 c. corn bread stuffing mix
1 c. sour cream
12 thin slices boiled ham
3 tbsp. butter, melted
3 tbsp. flour
1 1/2 c. milk
1/4 c. shredded Cheddar cheese
2 tbsp. Parmesan cheese

Combine . . . . first 3 ingredients in bowl, mixing well.
Spread . . . . . evenly over ham slices, rolling to enclose filling.
Arrange . . . . . seam side down in single layer in shallow baking pan.
Blend . . . . . . butter and flour in saucepan.
Stir . . . . in milk gradually.
Cook . . . . until thick and bubbly, stirring constantly.
Add . . . . Cheddar cheese; remove from heat and stir until cheese is melted.
Pour . . . . over ham rolls.
Sprinkle . . . . with Parmesan cheese.
Bake . . . . covered, at 350 degrees for 15 minutes.
Bake . . . . uncovered, for 15 minutes longer.
Yields . . . . . . 6 servings.

Ruth Ballif
Xi Nu Zeta, Newhall, California

MOM'S COMPANY PORK CHOPS

4 lg. potatoes, peeled, sliced
1/4 lb. Velveeta cheese, diced
1 1/2 c. milk
Salt and pepper to taste

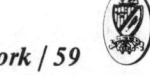

4 lg. pork chops
Flour

Arrange ..... potato slices on bottom of 2 1/2-quart flat baking dish.
Top .... with cheese, milk, salt and pepper.
Coat ...... pork chops with flour, seasoning to taste.
Arrange ..... over potato mixture.
Bake .... at 350 degrees for 1 1/2 hours.
Yields ...... 4 servings.

Cindy Standridge
Zeta Theta, Lindsay, Oklahoma

PORK CHOPS-CARROTS-POTATO CASSEROLE

4 to 6 pork chops, trimmed
Salt and pepper to taste
4 or 5 med. potatoes, peeled, sliced
4 or 5 carrots, peeled, sliced
1 can tomato soup

Season ..... pork chops with salt and pepper.
Brown ...... in a small amount of oil in skillet.
Layer ...... pork chops, potatoes and carrots in 2-quart casserole.
Pour .... soup over top.
Bake .... at 350 degrees for 1 hour or until tender.
Yields ...... 2-4 servings.

Barbara A. Williams
Alpha Psi, Sidney, Montana

PORK-SAUERKRAUT CASSEROLE

6 pork chops
Salt and pepper to taste
1 lg. can sauerkraut
3 med. potatoes, peeled, quartered
3 apples, quartered
12 prunes
2 carrots, scraped, sliced
3 stalks celery, cut into
    1 1/2-in. pieces
1/4 tsp. minced onion

Season ..... pork chops with salt and pepper.
Brown ...... in skillet.
Layer ...... sauerkraut, pork chops and remaining ingredients in order given in baking dish.

Bake .... covered, at 375 degrees for 1 hour.
Yields ...... 6 servings.

Mildred Vacek
Xi Theta Zeta, Dickinson, Texas

SPANISH PORK CHOPS

4 to 6 pork chops
2 med. onions, chopped
1 lg. green pepper, chopped
1 1/2 c. long grain rice
1   16-oz. can tomatoes
1 can beef broth
1   6-oz. can tomato paste
1 1/2 tsp. salt
1 tsp. sugar
1/2 tsp. pepper
1 c. shredded sharp cheese

Brown ...... pork chops with onions and green pepper in skillet.
Add .... rice.
Saute ...... until lightly browned.
Stir .... in next 6 ingredients and 4 cups water.
Simmer ..... covered, for 1 hour and 20 minutes.
Sprinkle .... cheese over top.
Simmer ..... covered, for 10 minutes longer.
Yields ...... 4-6 servings.

Anita Wilson
Preceptor Beta Zeta, Mansfield, Ohio

WILD RICE CASSEROLE

Pork chops
2 c. rice
2 cans beef broth
1 stick margarine, melted
4 tbsp. each green pepper, celery,
    shallots
1 tbsp. Worcestershire sauce

Brown ...... pork chops in skillet; drain.
Combine .... with remaining 7 ingredients and 1 broth can water in casserole.
Bake .... at 375 degrees for 1 hour or until liquid is absorbed.
Let .... stand, covered, for 5 minutes before serving.
Yields ...... 6-8 servings.

Lucy D. Allen
Xi Gamma Pi, La Place, Louisiana

SCALLOPED POTATOES AND PORK CHOPS SUPREME

6 lean pork chops
10 med. potatoes, thinly sliced
2 cans cream of mushroom soup
1 can evaporated milk
2 c. milk
1 med. onion, chopped
1 tsp. salt
1/2 tsp. pepper
Butter
2 c. crushed potato chips

Cook . . . . pork chops in 1/4 cup water in skillet until water evaporates and chops brown.
Layer . . . . . . potatoes in bottom of 9 x 12-inch baking dish.
Combine . . . . remaining ingredients except butter and potato chips in bowl, mixing well.
Pour . . . . over potatoes.
Arrange . . . . . pork chops on top.
Dot . . . . each with butter.
Top . . . . with potato chips.
Bake . . . . covered with vented foil, at 350 degrees for 1 1/2 hours.
Yields . . . . . . 6 servings.

Bobbie Hand
Lambda Eta, Saline, Michigan

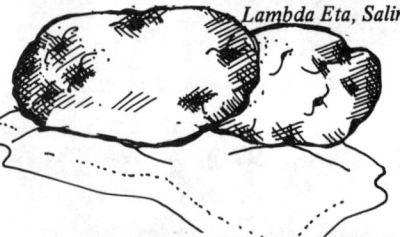

BAKED PORK CHOP CASSEROLE

1   9-oz. package frozen French-style green beans
Salt
2 tbsp. flour
3 tbsp. margarine, melted
1 1/2 c. milk
1   6-oz. package long grain and wild rice, cooked
1 .5-oz. can sliced water chestnuts
Pepper
6   1-in. thick pork chops

Combine . . . . beans with boiling salted water in saucepan.
Bring . . . . to a boil; drain.
Blend . . . . . . flour with margarine in saucepan.
Stir . . . . in milk gradually.
Cook . . . . until thick, stirring constantly.
Combine . . . . with rice, beans, water chestnuts and 3/4 teaspoon pepper in bowl, mixing well.
Brown . . . . . . pork chops in skillet.
Season . . . . . to taste.
Place . . . . half the rice mixture in baking pan.
Layer . . . . . . pork chops and remaining rice mixture over top.
Bake . . . . covered, at 325 degrees for 1 hour and 25 minutes.
Yields . . . . . . 6 servings.

Jody Quincey
Xi Iota Upsilon, Ft. Lauderdale, Florida

PORK TENDERLOIN CASSEROLE

2 pork tenderloins, sliced 1/4 to 1/2 in. thick
Salt and pepper to taste
1 clove of garlic, minced
Butter
2 or 3 slices bacon, chopped
2 to 4 leeks, chopped
1 beef bouillon cube
2 tomatoes, sliced
1/2 lb. mushrooms, sliced

Brown . . . . . . tenderloin slices with salt, pepper and garlic in a small amount of butter in large skillet.
Cook . . . . bacon with leeks in a small amount of butter in small skillet until crisp.
Add . . . . to tenderloin mixture.
Stir . . . . in bouillon cube dissolved in 1 1/2 cups boiling water.
Top . . . . with tomato slices.
Cook . . . . covered, for 30 minutes or until tender.
Saute . . . . . . mushrooms in a small amount of butter in skillet.
Stir . . . . into pork mixture before serving.
Yields . . . . . . 6-8 servings.

Roberta Johansen
Preceptor Iota
Prince George, British Columbia, Canada

SPARERIBS WITH KRAUT

3 lb. spareribs, cut into pieces
2 tsp. salt
1/4 tsp. pepper
1   29-oz. can sauerkraut
2 med. carrots, shredded
1 1/2 c. tomato juice
2 tbsp. brown sugar
2 to 3 tsp. caraway seed
1 tart apple, finely chopped

Season ..... spareribs with salt and pepper.
Combine .... remaining ingredients in large bowl, mixing well.
Spread ..... in large baking pan.
Place .... spareribs meat side up on top.
Bake .... covered, at 350 degrees for 2 1/2 to 3 1/2 hours or until spareribs are tender, basting occasionally with pan juices.
Yields ...... 4-6 servings.

Nancy Cooper
Preceptor Laureate Alpha Pi, Arlington, Texas

BRUNCH EGG AND SAUSAGE CASSEROLE

1 lb. sausage
12 eggs, well beaten
1 can mushroom soup
1/2 c. milk
1/4 lb. Cheddar cheese, grated

Brown ...... sausage in skillet, stirring until crumbly; drain and remove.
Scramble .... eggs in a small amount of pan drippings until partially set.
Mix .... soup and milk in bowl.
Layer ...... sausage and eggs in 1 1/2-quart rectangular casserole.
Top .... with soup mixture and cheese.
Bake .... at 350 degrees until cheese is melted.
Yields ...... 8 servings.

Carole Walser
Xi Nu Lambda, Richardson, Texas

MACARONI AND SAUSAGE BAKE

1 lb. sausage
1 c. chopped onion
1   6-oz. package macaroni, cooked

1 can cream of mushroom soup
2/3 c. milk
3 eggs, slightly beaten
1/2 lb. sharp cheese, shredded
2 c. corn flakes, crushed
1 tbsp. butter, melted

Brown ...... sausage with onion in skillet, stirring until crumbly.
Layer ...... sausage mixture and macaroni in 8-inch square baking dish.
Combine .... soup and milk in saucepan, mixing well.
Cook .... over low heat until heated through.
Stir .... a small amount of hot soup into eggs; stir eggs into soup.
Add .... cheese, mixing well.
Pour .... over macaroni.
Toss .... corn flakes with butter.
Sprinkle .... over top.
Bake .... at 350 degrees for 40 to 45 minutes or until bubbly.

Rhonda Shuman
Zeta Theta, Lindsay, Oklahoma

QUICK SAUSAGE SUPPER

3/4 to 1 lb. sausage
1/2 c. chopped onion
2 tbsp. flour
1   16-oz. can tomatoes
1   4-oz. can mushroom stems and pieces
1 tsp. oregano
1/2 tsp. basil
1/4 tsp. garlic powder
1/8 tsp. pepper
10 refrigerator biscuits, quartered
1 c. shredded mozzarella cheese

Brown ...... sausage with onion in Dutch oven, stirring until crumbly; drain.
Sprinkle .... with flour.
Stir .... in vegetables and seasonings.
Cook .... until slightly thickened, stirring constantly.
Simmer ..... for several minutes.
Top .... with biscuits.
Sprinkle .... cheese over top.
Bake .... at 400 degrees for 12 to 16 minutes or until golden brown.

Kathy M. Kessler
Kappa Delta, Emporia, Kansas

BAKED SCALLOPED CORN AND SAUSAGE

1 lb. pork sausage
2 eggs
1 c. milk
1 tsp. salt
1 16-oz. can whole kernel corn,
   drained
2 c. soft bread crumbs
1 3/4-oz. envelope pork gravy mix

Brown . . . . . . sausage in skillet, stirring until
               crumbly; drain.
Beat . . . . eggs, milk and salt together in
               bowl.
Stir . . . . in sausage, corn and bread
               crumbs.
Spoon . . . . . . into shallow 1 1/2-quart baking
               dish.
Bake . . . . at 400 degrees for 15 to 20 min-
               utes or until knife inserted in
               center comes out clean.
Prepare . . . . . gravy mix using package
               directions.
Serve . . . . over casserole.
Yields . . . . . . 5-6 servings.

Frances E. Brillian
Xi Delta, Rochester, New York

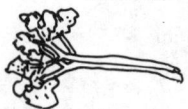

SCRUMPTIOUS SAUSAGE CASSEROLE

1 lb. pork sausage
1/2 c. chopped onion
1 can cream of chicken soup
3/4 c. milk
1/2 tsp. celery salt
1/2 tsp. salt
Dash of pepper
1 7-oz. package elbow macaroni,
   cooked, drained
1 17-oz. can peas, drained
1/2 c. slivered toasted almonds

Brown . . . . . . sausage and onion in skillet, stir-
               ring until crumbly.
Stir . . . . in remaining ingredients.
Spoon . . . . . . into casserole.
Bake . . . . at 350 degrees for 30 minutes.
Yields . . . . . . 8 servings.

Photograph for this recipe on page 55.

SKILLET SUPPER

1 lb. sausage
6 c. shredded cabbage
1 tsp. salt
1/2 tsp. caraway seed
Dash of pepper
2 c. cooked noodles
1 c. applesauce

Brown . . . . . . sausage in skillet, stirring until
               crumbly; drain.
Stir . . . . in next 4 ingredients.
Cook . . . . covered, for 10 minutes.
Add . . . . noodles and applesauce, mixing
               well.
Cook . . . . for 1 minute longer, stirring
               constantly.
Yields . . . . . . 4 servings.

June B. Fuller
Preceptor Beta Eta, Bradenton, Florida

EASY CASSOULET

1/2 lb. sausage
1 sm. onion, sliced
1 clove of garlic, minced
2 15-oz. cans navy beans
1 1/2 c. chopped cooked ham
1/4 c. dry white wine
2 tbsp. chopped parsley
1 bay leaf

Brown . . . . . . sausage with onion and garlic in
               skillet, stirring until crumbly;
               drain.
Combine . . . . with remaining ingredients in
               1 1/2-quart casserole, mixing
               well.
Bake . . . . covered, at 325 degrees for 45
               minutes.
Bake . . . . uncovered, for 40 to 45 minutes
               longer· or until cooked through,
               stirring occasionally; remove bay
               leaf.
Yields . . . . . . 6 servings.

Emily Baker
Xi Xi Mu, Bakersfield, California

SAUSAGE TANGO CASSEROLE

1 eggplant, cut into 1-in. cubes
1 lb. sausage

1 pkg. dry onion soup mix
1 can Spanish rice
1 can tomatoes
1 can mushrooms
1/3 c. chopped green pepper
1 c. grated Velveeta cheese
1/2 c. soft bread crumbs

Cook . . . . eggplant in 1 cup boiling water in saucepan for 10 minutes or until tender; drain.
Brown . . . . . . sausage in skillet, stirring until crumbly.
Combine . . . . eggplant, sausage and next 5 ingredients in greased casserole, mixing well.
Mix . . . . cheese and bread crumbs.
Sprinkle . . . . over casserole.
Garnish . . . . . with paprika.
Bake . . . . at 350 degrees for 30 minutes.

Syble Barnes
Delta Theta, Lexington, Missouri

SHIPWRECK

2 lb. sausage
1/2 c. rice
Salt and pepper to taste
4 lg. potatoes, sliced
2 or 3 med. onions, sliced
2 cans kidney beans, partially drained
1 can each mushroom, tomato soup

Brown . . . . . . sausage in skillet, stirring until crumbly; drain.
Stir . . . . in rice, salt and pepper.
Layer . . . . . . potatoes, onions, sausage mixture, beans, mushroom soup and tomato soup in large baking dish.
Bake . . . . covered, at 325 degrees for 2 to 2 1/2 hours or until vegetables are tender.
Yields . . . . . . 10-12 servings.

Cheryl Newham
Pi Psi, Richmond, Missouri

SUE'S ITALIAN CASSEROLE

1 1/2 lb. Italian sausage
1/2 c. each chopped onion, green pepper
1 4-oz. can mushrooms, drained
Butter
1 can stewed tomatoes

1 8-oz. can tomato sauce
1/4 lb. pepperoni, sliced
1/4 tsp. basil
1 1/2 c. cooked macaroni
1 8-oz. package shredded mozzarella cheese

Brown . . . . . . sausage in skillet, stirring until crumbly.
Saute . . . . . . onion, green pepper and mushrooms in a small amount of butter in skillet.
Combine . . . . with sausage and next 5 ingredients in 3-quart casserole, mixing well.
Bake . . . . covered, at 350 degrees for 1 hour.
Sprinkle . . . . cheese over top.
Bake . . . . uncovered, for 10 minutes longer.
Yields . . . . . . 6 servings.

Nancy L. Abbott
Preceptor Epsilon, Jamestown, New York

SAUSAGE MOSTACCIOLI

1 lb. smoked sausage links, cut into chunks
1/2 c. each chopped onion, green pepper
1 16-oz. can tomatoes
1 6-oz. can tomato paste
1/2 tsp. salt
1/4 tsp. each pepper, oregano
8 oz. curly macaroni, cooked
1/2 lb. sharp Cheddar cheese, grated
Parmesan cheese

Brown . . . . . . sausage in skillet; remove sausage.
Saute . . . . . . onion and green pepper in pan drippings until tender.
Stir . . . . in next 5 ingredients and 1/2 cup water.
Layer . . . . . . half the macaroni, sausage, tomato mixture and cheese in 2-quart casserole.
Repeat . . . . . layers with remaining ingredients.
Top . . . . with Parmesan cheese.
Bake . . . . at 350 degrees for 30 minutes.
Yields . . . . . . 6-8 servings.

Leilani Thomas
Xi Zeta Zeta, Colby, Kansas

EGGS PORTUGAL

1 1/2 lb. skinless sausage links, cut
   into thirds
8 slices white bread, trimmed, cubed
3/4 lb. sharp Cheddar cheese, grated
4 eggs, beaten
2 1/2 c. milk
2 1/4 tsp. prepared mustard
1 can cream of mushroom soup
1/4 c. vermouth
1 4 1/2-oz. can sliced mushrooms,
   drained

Brown . . . . . . sausage in skillet.
Layer . . . . . . bread cubes, cheese and sausage
           in lightly greased 9 x 13-inch
           baking dish.
Mix . . . . eggs, milk and mustard in bowl.
Pour . . . . over sausage.
Chill . . . . overnight.
Combine . . . . remaining 3 ingredients in bowl,
           mixing well.
Pour . . . . over casserole.
Bake . . . . at 300 degrees for 1 1/2 hours.
Yields . . . . . . 8-10 servings.

Martha Bunker
Preceptor Delta Pi, San Clemente, California

LINK SOUFFLE

1 1/2 lb. sausage links, cut into
   bite-sized pieces
4 eggs, beaten
1/2 tsp. dry mustard
1 1/2 c. milk
8 slices bread, cubed
1 1/2 c. grated Cheddar cheese
1 can cream of mushroom soup
1 4-oz. can mushrooms

Brown . . . . . . sausage in skillet; drain on paper
           towel.
Combine . . . . with remaining ingredients in
           greased 2 1/2-quart casserole,
           mixing well.
Bake . . . . covered, at 325 degrees for 1 1/2
           hours.
Yields . . . . . . 6-8 servings.

Judy Rummel
Alpha Phi, Hamilton, Montana

CORN BREAD-TOPPED CASSEROLE

1 lb. Polish sausage, cut into pieces
1 17-oz. can corn, drained
1 c. frozen green beans
1 8-oz. can stewed tomatoes
2 tbsp. butter
Salt and pepper to taste
1 10-oz. package corn bread mix

Place . . . . sausage in 1 1/2-quart baking
           dish.
Combine . . . . vegetables in bowl, mixing well.
Spoon . . . . . . over sausage.
Dot . . . . with butter.
Season . . . . . with salt and pepper.
Mix . . . . corn bread mix using package
           directions.
Spoon . . . . . . corn bread batter over all.
Bake . . . . at 425 degrees for 25 to 30 min-
           utes or until golden brown.
Yields . . . . . . 5-6 servings.

Darlene Rhodes
Xi Nu, Owensboro, Kentucky

POLISH SAUSAGE ROLL-UPS

1 c. minute rice
1 sm. green pepper, chopped
1 sm. onion, chopped
2 lb. Polish sausage, cut into
   4-in. pieces
1 pkg. sliced mozzarella cheese,
   cut in half
8 lasagna noodles, cooked
1 jar spaghetti sauce
Parmesan cheese

Cook . . . . rice using package directions and
           adding green pepper and onion.
Spread . . . . . in 9 x 13-inch baking dish.
Slit . . . . each piece sausage lengthwise
           and place 1 piece cheese in slit.
Roll . . . . up in noodles.
Arrange . . . . over rice mixture.
Spoon . . . . . . spaghetti sauce over roll-ups.
Top . . . . with Parmesan cheese.
Bake . . . . at 350 degrees for 30 minutes or
           until cooked through.
Yields . . . . . . 8 servings.

Harriet Duncan
Xi Alpha Delta, Bedford, Indiana

Poultry

BASQUE GARBANZO CASSEROLE

1/2 lb. pepperoni, sliced
1 chicken breast, boned, cut into
   2-in. pieces
1 lg. leek, chopped
2 cloves of garlic, minced
4 med. carrots, sliced
2 c. shredded cabbage
2　20-oz. cans garbanzo beans, drained
1　16-oz. can tomatoes
1 tbsp. salt
1 tsp. thyme
1/2 tsp. pepper

Saute ...... pepperoni in skillet for 5 min-
        utes; remove pepperoni.
Brown ...... chicken in pan drippings; remove
        chicken.
Saute ..... leek and garlic in pan drippings.
Stir .... in carrots.
Cook ...... for 3 minutes.
Add ...... cabbage, mixing well.
Cook ...... for 2 minutes.
Stir .... in remaining ingredients, pep-
        peroni and chicken, mixing well.
Spoon ..... into 3-quart baking dish.
Bake .... covered, at 325 degrees for 1
        hour.
Yields ..... 8 servings.

Catherine A. Vavra
Eta Mu, Kennesaw, Georgia

CHICKEN CUTLETS PARMESAN

4 chicken breasts, boned, cut into strips
2 eggs, beaten
2 c. Italian-style bread crumbs
1 jar spaghetti sauce
1 pkg. mozzarella cheese slices, cut
   into strips
Parmesan cheese

Dip .... chicken strips in egg in bowl.
Roll .... in bread crumbs.
Brown ...... in a small amount of oil in skil-
        let, stirring frequently; drain on
        paper towel.
Cook .... spaghetti sauce in saucepan until
        heated through.
Layer ...... sauce, chicken and mozzarella
        cheese alternately in baking dish
        until all ingredients are used.

Sprinkle .... with Parmesan cheese.
Bake .... at 325 degrees for 15 minutes.
Yields ...... 4 servings.

Susan Marcotte
Kappa, Auburn, Maine

CHICKEN AND RICE

1 1/2 c. minute rice
1 can each cream of mushroom, celery
   soup
1 c. milk
8 chicken breast halves, skinned
1/2 pkg. dry onion soup mix

Mix .... first 4 ingredients in 9 x 13-inch
        casserole.
Layer ...... chicken and soup mix over rice
        mixture.
Bake .... tightly covered, at 350 degrees
        for 2 hours.
Yields ..... 8 servings.

Betty Race
Laureate Lambda, Wichita, Kansas

SHERRIED CHICKEN

4 chicken breasts
1 c. flour
1 tsp. salt
1/2 tsp. paprika
1/2 c. melted butter
1 can cream of mushroom soup
1 sm. can mushrooms
1/2 c. cream Sherry

Coat .... chicken breasts with flour sea-
        soned with salt and paprika.
Place .... skin side down in butter in 9 x
        12-inch baking dish.
Bake .... at 325 degrees for 1/2 hour;
        turn.
Mix .... remaining 3 ingredients in bowl.
Pour .... half the soup mixture over
        chicken.
Bake .... for 30 minutes; turn.
Pour .... remaining soup mixture over
        chicken.
Bake .... for 30 to 45 minutes longer or
        until tender.
Yields ...... 4 servings.

Peggy Bertolet
Preceptor Nu, Phoenix, Arizona

CREAMY CHICKEN CASSEROLE

2 10-oz. packages frozen broccoli,
    cooked
6 chicken breasts, cooked, boned
2 c. milk
2 8-oz. packages cream cheese, softened
1 1/2 c. Parmesan cheese
1 tsp. garlic salt
Bread crumbs (opt.)

Layer ...... broccoli and chicken in greased
            2-quart casserole.
Cook .... milk, cream cheese, 1 cup Par-
            mesan cheese and garlic salt in
            saucepan over low heat until
            cheese is melted, stirring
            constantly.
Pour .... over chicken.
Top .... with remaining Parmesan cheese
            and bread crumbs.
Bake .... at 350 degrees for 30 to 35 min-
            utes or until bubbly.
Yields ...... 12-15 servings.

Lou Ann Legati
Alpha Iota, Ocean Springs, Mississippi

SPICY CHICKEN BAKE

1 8-oz. bottle of Russian
    salad dressing
1 c. orange marmalade
1 pkg. dry onion soup mix
6 to 8 chicken breasts

Mix .... first 3 ingredients in bowl.
Place .... chicken in baking dish.
Cover ...... with sauce.
Chill .... overnight.
Bake .... at 350 degrees for 45 minutes,
            basting occasionally.
Yields ...... 6-8 servings.

Juanita M. Norwood
Preceptor Beta Theta, Lee's Summit, Missouri

PUFFED CHICKEN RICOTTA

2 whole chicken breasts, halved,
    skinned, boned
1/2 tsp. salt
1/4 tsp. white pepper
3 tbsp. butter, melted
1/2 c. ricotta cheese

1/4 c. orange juice
2 tsp. grated orange rind
1/2 tsp. rosemary
1 sheet frozen puff pastry, thawed
1 egg, beaten

Cook .... chicken seasoned with salt and
            pepper in butter in skillet over
            medium heat for 3 minutes on
            each side or until lightly
            browned.
Mix .... next 4 ingredients in small bowl.
Cut .... pastry sheet into 4 squares.
Roll .... each square on lightly floured
            surface large enough to enclose
            chicken breast.
Place .... chicken breasts on pastry and
            spread with cheese mixture,
            wrapping to enclose filling; seal
            edges.
Place .... on baking sheet.
Brush ...... with egg.
Bake .... at 350 degrees for 20 minutes or
            until golden brown.
Yields ...... 4 servings.

Emily A. Mullis
Preceptor Sigma, Rome, Georgia

MAKE-AHEAD COMPANY CHICKEN

8 oz. tomato sauce
1/4 c. honey
1/4 c. mustard
1 tsp. Worcestershire sauce
10 to 12 chicken thighs and breasts

Combine .... first 4 ingredients in bowl, mix-
            ing well.
Spoon ...... into 9 x 11-inch baking pan.
Place .... chicken skin side down in sauce.
Bake .... at 350 degrees for 30 to 40 min-
            utes; turn.
Bake .... for 30 to 40 minutes longer or
            until tender; cool.
Chill .... covered, overnight.
Bake .... covered, at 350 degrees for 20 to
            25 minutes or until heated
            through, basting frequently.
Bake .... uncovered, at 400 degrees for 10
            to 15 minutes or until crisp.
Yields ...... 8-10 servings.

Meda Uker
Preceptor Iota, Omaha, Nebraska

FANCY CHICKEN

4 chicken breasts, boned
1 2.5-oz. package smoked sliced beef
8 slices bacon
1 can cream of mushroom soup
1/4 c. sour cream
1/4 c. vermouth

Fold .... each chicken breast around 3 slices beef.
Wrap .... 2 slices bacon around each chicken breast.
Place .... seam side down in 9 x 9-inch baking pan.
Bake .... at 350 degrees for 1/2 hour; drain.
Mix .... remaining 3 ingredients in bowl.
Pour .... over chicken.
Bake .... at 325 degrees for 1 hour.
Serve .... over rice.
Yields ...... 4 servings.

Lynn Burkley
Xi Xi Mu, Bakersfield, California

BARBECUED CHICKEN CASSEROLE

1 3 to 3 1/2-lb. chicken, cut up
1/2 c. flour
2 tsp. salt
1/2 c. oil
1 med. onion, sliced
1/2 c. chopped celery
1/4 c. minced green pepper
1 c. catsup
2 tbsp. Worcestershire sauce
2 tbsp. brown sugar
1/8 tsp. pepper
1 pkg. frozen cut corn (opt.)

Coat .... chicken with flour seasoned with salt.
Brown ...... in oil in skillet.
Place .... chicken in 3-quart casserole.
Saute ...... onion in 2 tablespoons pan drippings until golden.
Add .... 1 cup water and next 6 ingredients, mixing well.
Pour .... over chicken.
Chill .... for several hours.
Bake .... covered, at 350 degrees for 1 hour and 20 minutes.
Top .... with corn.

Bake .... covered, for 25 minutes longer or until chicken is tender.
Yields ...... 6 servings.

Helen R. Johnson
Preceptor Omicron, Niagara Falls, New York

BAKED ALMOND-CHICKEN CASSEROLE

3 c. chopped cooked chicken
1 1/2 c. chopped celery
1 c. salad dressing
1 c. finely chopped Swiss cheese
1/4 c. chopped onion
2 tbsp. chopped pimento
1 tsp. salt
Dash of pepper
1/2 c. slivered almonds, toasted
1 tomato, cut into wedges

Combine .... first 8 ingredients and 1/4 cup almonds in bowl, mixing well.
Spoon ...... into 6 x 10-inch baking dish.
Sprinkle .... with remaining almonds.
Bake .... at 350 degrees for 25 minutes.
Top .... with tomato.
Bake .... for 5 minutes longer.
Yields ...... 4-6 servings.

Linda Sanders
Gamma Sigma, Raleigh, North Carolina

BAKED CHICKEN WITH BRAN

2 c. Bran Chex, crushed
1 med. onion, sliced, separated
into rings
1 4-oz. can sliced mushrooms
3 lb. chicken parts
2 tbsp. Worcestershire sauce
1 c. milk
1 can cream of mushroom soup

Place .... Bran Chex in bottom of 9 x 13-inch baking pan.
Top .... with half the onion, all the mushrooms, chicken parts skin side up and remaining onion.
Mix .... 1 cup water, Worcestershire sauce, milk and soup in saucepan.
Cook ...... until heated through.

Pour . . . . over chicken.
Bake . . . . at 400 degrees for 1 1/2 hours or
until chicken is tender.
Yields . . . . . . 4-6 servings.

Janet H. Tubbs
X-477-XAE, Cincinnati, Ohio

BAKED CHICKEN SALAD

1 c. crushed potato chips
2/3 c. shredded sharp Cheddar cheese
4 c. chopped cooked chicken
2 c. chopped celery
2 tbsp. chopped onion
1/2 c. slivered almonds
1 tsp. salt
3/4 c. mayonnaise
1 can cream of chicken soup
2 tbsp. lemon juice
2 pimentos, chopped
4 hard-boiled eggs, sliced

Mix . . . . potato chips and cheese in bowl.
Combine . . . . half the cheese mixture with
next 9 ingredients, mixing well.
Spoon . . . . . . into shallow 1 1/2-quart baking
dish.
Arrange . . . . . eggs on top.
Sprinkle . . . . with remaining cheese mixture.
Chill . . . . for several hours.
Bake . . . . at 400 degrees for 25 minutes or
until heated through.
May . . . . substitute sunflower seed or
water chestnuts for almonds.
Yields . . . . . . 8-9 servings.

Erma Brown
Beta Sigma Phi XP1587, Marshall, Missouri

CALIFORNIA CASSEROLE

2 cans boned chicken
1 pkg. frozen California Blend vegetables
1 can sliced water chestnuts, drained
1 c. shredded Cheddar cheese
2 cans cream of mushroom soup

Combine . . . . all ingredients in baking dish,
mixing well.
Garnish . . . . . with slivered almonds.
Bake . . . . at 350 degrees for 45 minutes.

Jeanne Holden
Preceptor Eta, Menomonie, Wisconsin

EL RANCHO CHICKEN

1 lg. package potato chips, crushed
3 c. chopped cooked chicken
1 c. chopped celery
2 hard-boiled eggs, chopped
1 8-oz. can water chestnuts, sliced
1 c. mayonnaise
1/4 to 1/2 c. chicken broth
Butter

Place . . . . half the potato chips over bot-
tom of 6 x 10-inch baking dish.
Mix . . . . next 6 ingredients in bowl.
Spoon . . . . . . over potato chips.
Top . . . . with remaining potato chips.
Dot . . . . with butter.
Garnish . . . . . with parsley flakes and paprika.
Bake . . . . covered, at 350 degrees for 30
minutes.
Bake . . . . uncovered, for 15 minutes
longer.
Yields . . . . . . 4 servings.

Gloria Smethers
Preceptor Theta, Beatrice, Nebraska

SHERRY'S CHICKEN ENCHILADAS

1 chicken, cooked, chopped
1 can green chilies, chopped
1/2 lb. mild Cheddar cheese, grated
1/2 lb. Monterey Jack cheese, grated
12 tortillas
1 can cream of chicken soup
1 8-oz. carton sour cream

Combine . . . . chicken, chilies and half the
cheeses in bowl, mixing well.
Soften . . . . . . tortillas in a small amount of oil
in skillet; drain.
Spoon . . . . . . chicken mixture onto tortillas,
rolling to enclose filling.
Place . . . . seam side down in 9 x 13-inch
baking dish.
Combine . . . . soup, sour cream and remaining
cheeses in bowl, mixing well.
Spoon . . . . . . over tortillas.
Bake . . . . covered, at 350 degrees for 35
minutes or until cheese is
melted.
Yields . . . . . . 6 servings.

Sherry Blackwell
Delta Epsilon Epsilon, Arroya Grande, California

CHICKEN FRICASSEE

2 c. chopped cooked chicken
1/2 c. chopped celery
1/4 c. chopped onion
1/4 c. mayonnaise
2 eggs, beaten
1 1/2 c. milk
Salt and pepper to taste
6 slices bread, toasted, buttered, cubed
2 slices bread, toasted, cubed
1 can mushroom soup

Combine .... first 8 ingredients in bowl, mixing well.
Layer ...... buttered bread cubes, chicken mixture and unbuttered bread cubes in 8 x 13-inch casserole.
Chill .... overnight.
Top .... with soup.
Bake .... at 350 degrees for 1 hour.
Yields ...... 6 servings.

Jessie Neier
Xi Epsilon Psi, Seelyville, Indiana

CHICKEN TORTE

1 lg. chicken
4 eggs, beaten
1 c. milk
1/2 c. flour
2 lg. stalks celery, chopped
2 tbsp. chopped onion
Butter
8 slices bread, cubed
2 tsp. poultry seasoning
Buttered bread crumbs

Cook .... chicken with enough water to cover in saucepan until tender.
Bone .... and chop chicken, reserving skin and broth.
Put .... skin through food grinder.
Add .... enough reserved broth to measure 4 cups.
Mix .... in eggs, milk and flour.
Pour .... half into buttered baking dish.
Saute ...... celery and onion in 1/4 cup butter in skillet until tender.
Add .... bread and seasoning, mixing well.
Spoon ...... into baking dish.
Top .... with chicken, remaining broth mixture and bread crumbs.

Bake .... at 350 degrees for 1 hour.
Yields ...... 8 servings.

Lillian Dickens
Preceptor Beta Eta, Wichita, Kansas

VELVEETA CHICKEN

1 box chicken-flavored stuffing mix
1 can cream of chicken soup
6 oz. Velveeta cheese
1/2 can evaporated milk
1 chicken, baked, boned

Prepare ..... stuffing mix using package directions.
Combine .... next 3 ingredients in saucepan.
Cook .... until cheese is melted, stirring constantly.
Layer ...... chicken, cheese mixture and stuffing in 9 x 11-inch casserole.
Bake .... at 350 degrees for 1/2 hour.
Yields ...... 6 servings.

Mary Conrad
Gamma Iota, Chillicothe, Missouri

CHICKEN-VEGETABLE BAKE

1/2 c. flour
1 1/2 tsp. salt
1/4 tsp. pepper
1 tbsp. paprika
1 chicken, cut up
1/4 c. oil
1 8-oz. can whole onions, drained
1/2 c. chopped carrots
1 3-oz. can sliced mushrooms, drained
1 tbsp. brown sugar
1/4 tsp. ginger
3 oz. frozen orange juice concentrate, thawed

Combine .... first 4 ingredients in plastic bag.
Add .... 2 or 3 pieces of chicken at a time, shaking to coat; reserve 2 tablespoons seasoned flour.
Brown ...... chicken in oil in skillet; remove to 2-quart casserole.
Add .... onions, carrots and mushrooms.
Blend ...... reserved flour, brown sugar, ginger and dash of salt into pan drippings.
Add .... orange juice concentrate and 3/4 cup water.

Cook . . . . until smooth, stirring constantly.
Pour . . . . over chicken.
Bake . . . . covered, at 350 degrees for 1 1/4 hours.
Yields . . . . . . 4 servings.

Teresa C. Piper
Delta Eta Gamma, Huntington Beach, California

CHICKEN ENCORE

14 oz. chopped cooked chicken
1 8-oz. package elbow macaroni
2 cans cream of mushroom soup
4 hard-boiled eggs, chopped
1 med. onion, chopped
1 c. milk
1 c. chicken broth
1/2 lb. mild cheese, cubed

Combine . . . . all ingredients in 9 x 13-inch baking dish, mixing well.
Chill . . . . covered, overnight.
Bake . . . . at 350 degrees for 1 hour.
Yields . . . . . . 8-12 servings.

Dorothy J. Burley
Xi Mu, Van Wert, Ohio

EASY CHICKEN CASSEROLE

2 to 3 c. chopped cooked chicken
2 c. shell macaroni
2 c. milk
1 can each cream of chicken,
mushroom soup
1 sm. onion, chopped
1 c. diced Velveeta cheese
1/2 c. chopped green pepper
1/2 c. chopped celery

Combine . . . . all ingredients in baking dish, mixing well.
Chill . . . . overnight.
Bake . . . . at 350 degrees for 1 hour.

Lori Ann Smith
Mu Lambda, Fairfax, Missouri

CHICKEN CREOLE CASSEROLE

1 med. onion, chopped
Butter
1 16-oz. jar spaghetti sauce

2 cans cream of chicken soup
1 sm. can evaporated milk
1 2 1/2 to 3 1/2-lb. chicken,
cooked, chopped
Salt and pepper to taste
12 oz. noodles, cooked
1/2 lb. Cheddar cheese, shredded

Saute . . . . . . onion in a small amount of butter in skillet until golden, stirring frequently.
Add . . . . spaghetti sauce and soup, mixing well; remove from heat.
Stir . . . . in next 4 ingredients.
Add . . . . noodles, tossing to mix.
Place . . . . in buttered 9 x 13-inch casserole.
Sprinkle . . . . cheese over top.
Bake . . . . at 375 degrees for 20 minutes or until bubbly.
Yields . . . . . . 6-8 servings.

Mary Magnus
Xi Gamma Mu, Springfield, Missouri

CHICKEN LASAGNA

1/2 c. each chopped onion, green pepper
3 tbsp. butter
1 can cream of chicken soup
1/3 c. milk
1 6-oz. can sliced mushrooms
1/4 c. chopped pimento
1/2 tsp. basil
8 oz. lasagna noodles, cooked
1 1/2 c. cream-style cottage cheese
8 oz. American cheese, shredded
1/2 c. Parmesan cheese
3 c. chopped cooked chicken

Saute . . . . . . onion and green pepper in butter in skillet until tender.
Stir . . . . in next 5 ingredients.
Layer . . . . . . half the noodles, soup mixture, cottage cheese, American cheese, Parmesan cheese and chicken in 9 x 13-inch baking pan.
Repeat . . . . . layers with remaining ingredients.
Bake . . . . at 350 degrees for 45 minutes.
Yields . . . . . . 8-10 servings.

Nancy Bircher
Xi Epsilon Theta, Ellsworth, Kansas

HOLIDAY CASSEROLE

1 6-oz. package noodles, cooked
1 can cream of chicken soup
1 6-oz. can evaporated milk
1 tsp. salt
1 1/2 c. shredded American cheese
2 c. chopped cooked chicken
1 c. finely chopped celery
1/4 c. finely chopped green pepper
1/4 c. finely chopped pimento
1 c. slivered blanched almonds

Spread ..... noodles over bottom and up sides of 2-quart casserole.
Combine .... soup, evaporated milk and salt in saucepan, mixing well.
Cook .... until heated through, stirring constantly.
Add .... cheese.
Cook ...... until cheese melts, stirring constantly.
Stir .... in remaining ingredients except almonds.
Pour .... over noodles.
Top .... with almonds.
Bake .... at 350 degrees for 30 minutes or until bubbly.
Yields ...... 8-10 servings.

Dorothy McDougall
Preceptor Gamma, St. Paul, Minnesota

CHICKEN TETRAZZINI DELUXE

1 med. onion, chopped
6 tbsp. butter
1/4 c. flour
1 1/2 c. chicken broth
1 c. heavy cream
1 tsp. salt
1/8 tsp. pepper
1/2 c. dry vermouth
3/4 c. Parmesan cheese
1/2 lb. mushrooms, sliced
12 oz. spaghetti, cooked
3 c. chopped cooked chicken

Saute ...... onion in 4 tablespoons butter in skillet until tender-crisp.
Blend ...... in flour.
Stir .... in broth and cream gradually.
Bring .... to a boil, stirring constantly.
Add .... next 3 ingredients and 1/4 cup cheese, mixing well.

Saute ...... mushrooms in 2 remaining tablespoons butter in skillet until brown.
Combine .... spaghetti, mushrooms and chicken in 2 1/2-quart casserole.
Top .... with sauce and remaining cheese.
Bake .... at 375 degrees for 20 minutes or until bubbly.
Yields ...... 6 servings.

Photograph for this recipe on page 65.

CHICKEN SPAGHETTI

2 med. onions, chopped
2 green peppers, chopped
2/3 c. chopped celery
1 med. can each English peas, tomatoes
2 cans mushroom soup
1 sm. jar pimentos, chopped
1 c. tomato juice
1 2-lb. package spaghetti, cooked
1 4 1/2 to 6-lb. chicken, cooked, boned
1 lb. mild Cheddar cheese, grated
Grated Velveeta cheese

Saute ...... first 3 ingredients in a small amount of oil in skillet until tender.
Drain ...... English peas, reserving liquid.
Add .... peas to sauteed vegetables with tomatoes, soup, pimentos and tomato juice, mixing well.
Combine .... spaghetti and chicken in large bowl, mixing well.
Stir .... in vegetables and Cheddar cheese.
Spoon ...... into large casserole.
Top .... with Velveeta cheese.
Bake .... at 350 degrees for 30 minutes or until bubbly, adding reserved liquid if necessary.
Yields ...... 20 servings.

Phyllis J. Barnes
Xi Pi Xi, Los Banos, California

EASY CHICKEN WITH RICE

2 c. rice
1 env. dry onion soup mix
1 can cream of mushroom soup
1 can mushroom pieces, drained
1 1/2 lb. chicken pieces

Salt and pepper to taste
Butter

Combine . . . . first 4 ingredients with 2 cups water in 8 x 10-inch casserole, mixing well.
Top . . . . with chicken.
Sprinkle . . . . chicken with salt and pepper and dot with butter.
Bake . . . . covered, at 350 degrees for 1 hour.
Bake . . . . uncovered, at 325 degrees for 15 minutes.
Yields . . . . . . 4-6 servings.

Teresa D. Hilgers
Xi Zeta, Decatur, Illinois

SLICK-CHICK CASSEROLE

1 can each cream of mushroom, chicken
  soup
1/2 soup can milk
1/2 tsp. onion powder
4 c. cooked rice
3 c. coarsely chopped cooked chicken
1 c. grated Cheddar cheese
2 tbsp. chopped pimento

Combine . . . . soups and milk in large saucepan, mixing well.
Cook . . . . until heated through, stirring constantly.
Stir . . . . in remaining ingredients.
Pour . . . . into greased 2-quart casserole.
Bake . . . . at 375 degrees for 25 to 30 minutes or until bubbly.
Yields . . . . . . 8 servings.

Sylvia Ann Cain
Beta Sigma Phi, Tweed, Ontario, Canada

COUNTRY CAPTAIN

1 c. rice
1 lg. chicken, cut up
Salt and pepper to taste
1/3 c. margarine, melted
1 med. green pepper, chopped
1 onion, chopped
1 clove of garlic, minced
1   19-oz. can tomatoes
2 to 3 tsp. curry powder
1 tsp. thyme
1/4 c. seedless raisins
1/2 c. chopped toasted almonds

Cook . . . . rice using package directions for half the cooking time.
Season . . . . . chicken with salt and pepper.
Cook . . . . in margarine in skillet until well browned.
Layer . . . . . . rice and chicken in 3-quart casserole.
Saute . . . . . . green pepper, onion and garlic in a small amount of pan drippings in skillet until tender-crisp.
Stir . . . . in remaining ingredients and salt to taste.
Bring . . . . to a boil.
Pour . . . . over chicken, stirring gently.
Bake . . . . covered, at 350 degrees for 1 hour or until chicken is tender.
Yields . . . . . . 4-6 servings.

Charlene K. Gibson
Xi Gamma Delta, Granada Hills, California

SYLVIA'S CHICKEN AND DUMPLINGS CASSEROLE

1   7-oz. can chicken, chopped
1 can cream of chicken soup
1/2 c. chopped celery
3/4 c. grated cheese
1/2 c. evaporated milk
1 egg
1/3 c. milk
2 tbsp. oil
1 c. flour
1 1/2 tsp. baking powder
1/2 tsp. salt

Combine . . . . first 5 ingredients in saucepan, mixing well.
Cook . . . . over medium heat until cheese is melted.
Pour . . . . into buttered 1 1/2-quart baking dish.
Mix . . . . egg, milk and oil in bowl.
Add . . . . remaining 3 ingredients, stirring until just moistened.
Drop . . . . by spoonfuls over chicken.
Bake . . . . covered, at 375 degrees for 20 to 25 minutes or until chicken is tender.
Bake . . . . uncovered, for 5 to 10 minutes longer or until dumplings are golden brown.

Alice L. Case
Beta Zeta, Ranchester, Wyoming

CHICKEN AND WILD RICE CASSEROLE

3 to 4 c. chopped cooked chicken
1 8-oz. carton chive dip
1/2 c. Cheddar cheese
1 c. chopped celery
1 c. chopped onion
1 can mushroom soup
1 lb. wild rice, cooked
1/2 c. milk
1 c. sliced water chestnuts

Combine .... all ingredients in 9 x 13-inch baking dish.
Garnish ..... with crushed potato chips.
Bake .... covered, for 30 minutes.
Bake .... uncovered, for 30 minutes longer or until celery is tender.
Yields ...... 8-10 servings.

Maurine Edmond
Xi Gamma Delta, Des Moines, Iowa

DEVONSHIRE CHICKEN

2 3-lb. chickens, cut up
Flour
Salt and pepper to taste
1 stick butter
3 onions, finely chopped
2 apples, peeled, chopped
1 c. chicken broth
1 1/2 c. unsweetened apple cider
1 c. cream

Dredge ..... chicken in flour seasoned with salt and pepper.
Brown ...... in butter in Dutch oven over moderately high heat; remove.
Saute ...... onions and apples in pan drippings until onions are tender.
Stir .... in 1/4 cup flour.
Cook .... over low heat for 2 minutes, stirring constantly.
Add .... broth, cider and chicken.
Bring .... to a boil, stirring constantly.
Bake .... covered, at 350 degrees for 35 to 40 minutes or until tender.
Remove .... chicken to serving plate.
Cook .... pan juices until slightly reduced, skimming if necessary.
Stir .... in cream and adjust seasonings.
Bring .... to a boil.

Spoon ...... over chicken.
Yields ...... 8-10 servings.

Grace Silvestro
Preceptor Iota Rho, Santa Rosa, California

CAREFREE CASSEROLE

1 10-oz. package frozen peas and carrots
1 can cream of mushroom soup
1/2 c. milk
3 c. cooked rice
1 1/2 c. chopped cooked turkey
Salt and pepper to taste
1/2 c. shredded American cheese

Combine .... first 3 ingredients and 1/2 cup water in saucepan.
Simmer ..... for 3 minutes.
Layer ...... half the vegetable mixture, all the rice, turkey, salt and pepper in 1 1/2-quart baking dish.
Top .... with remaining vegetable mixture and cheese.
Bake .... at 350 degrees for 20 minutes.
Yields ...... 6 servings.

Ann M. Clapper
Xi Zeta Psi, Shawnee-On-Delaware, Pennsylvania

EASY COMPANY CASSEROLE

4 c. coarsely chopped cooked turkey
2 14-oz. cans macaroni and cheese
1 c. sliced mushrooms
1 8-oz. can sliced water chestnuts, drained
1 2-oz. package slivered almonds
2 cans cream of chicken soup
1 1/2 c. shredded Cheddar cheese
1 c. herb-seasoned stuffing mix
6 tbsp. butter

Combine .... first 6 ingredients and 1 cup cheese in bowl, mixing well.
Spoon ...... into 9 x 13-inch baking dish.
Top .... with remaining cheese.
Saute ...... stuffing mix in butter in skillet for several minutes.
Layer ...... over cheese.
Bake .... at 350 degrees for 30 minutes.
Yields ...... 6-8 servings.

Vivian A. Hodges
Xi Epsilon Delta, Mt. Pleasant, Iowa

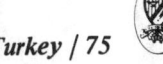

TURKEY DINNER FOR-A-CROWD

1 c. chopped onion
1/4 c. bacon drippings
8 slices crisp-cooked bacon, crumbled
2 10-oz. packages chopped spinach,
*   cooked, drained*
3 c. cooked rice
1/2 c. sliced celery
1/4 c. chopped pimento
2 cans cream of mushroom soup
1 c. sour cream
1 2-lb. boneless turkey roast, cooked
1 1/2 c. soft bread crumbs
2 tbsp. butter, melted

Saute .... onion in bacon drippings in skil-
               let until tender.
Add .... bacon, spinach, rice, celery and
               pimento, mixing well.
Combine .... soup and sour cream in bowl,
               stirring well.
Stir .... half the soup mixture into rice
               mixture.
Slice .... turkey into 12 portions.
Layer ...... half the rice mixture and turkey
               in 9 x 13-inch baking dish.
Top .... with remaining rice mixture and
               soup mixture.
Toss .... bread crumbs with butter.
Sprinkle .... over casserole.
Bake .... at 350 degrees for 35 to 40 min-
               utes or until golden brown.
Yields ...... 12 servings.

Janet Luedtke
Iota Phi, West Bend, Iowa

TURKEY AMANDZINI

3/4 c. mayonnaise
1/3 c. flour
2 tbsp. minced onion
1 tsp. garlic salt
2 1/4 c. milk
1 c. shredded Swiss cheese
1/3 c. dry white wine
7 oz. spaghetti, cooked, drained
2 c. chopped cooked turkey
1 10-oz. package frozen chopped broccoli,
*   thawed, drained*
1/4 c. chopped pimento
1 4-oz. can sliced mushrooms, drained
1 1/4 c. sliced almonds

Blend ...... first 4 ingredients in medium
               saucepan.
Stir .... in milk gradually.
Cook .... over low heat until thick, stirring
               constantly.
Stir .... in cheese and wine until cheese
               is melted.
Combine .... with next 5 ingredients and 3/4
               cup almonds in bowl, tossing to
               mix.
Spoon ...... into 8 x 12-inch baking dish.
Top .... with remaining 1/2 cup almonds.
Bake .... at 350 degrees for 40 to 45 min-
               utes or until heated through.
Serve ...... with Parmesan cheese.
Yields ...... 8-10 servings.

Ann P. Schenning
Preceptor Iota, Bel Air, Maryland

THREE-CHEESE TURKEY BAKE

1/2 c. each chopped onion, green pepper
3 tbsp. butter
1 can cream of chicken soup
1 4-oz. can sliced mushrooms, drained
1/2 c. chopped pimento
1/3 c. milk
1/2 tsp. basil
8 oz. lasagna noodles, cooked, drained
1 1/2 c. cottage cheese
2 c. chopped cooked turkey
1 1/2 c. shredded American cheese
1/2 c. Parmesan cheese

Saute ...... onion and green pepper in butter
               in skillet until tender.
Add .... next 5 ingredients, mixing well.
Layer ...... half the noodles, soup mixture,
               cottage cheese, turkey, Ameri-
               can and Parmesan cheeses in 9 x
               13-inch baking dish.
Repeat ..... layers with remaining ingredients
               except cheeses.
Bake .... at 350 degrees for 45 minutes.
Top .... with remaining cheeses.
Bake .... for 2 minutes longer or until
               cheese is melted.
Yields ...... 8 servings.

Estelle D. Seachrist
Preceptor Alpha Kappa, Fishersville, Virginia

TURKEY CRESCENT AMANDINE

3 c. chopped cooked turkey
1 can cream of mushroom soup
1 8-oz. can sliced water chestnuts, drained
1 4-oz. can sliced mushrooms, drained
2/3 c. mayonnaise
1/2 c. each chopped celery, onion
1 can refrigerator crescent rolls
2/3 c. shredded Swiss cheese
1/2 c. slivered almonds
4 tbsp. margarine, melted

Combine .... first 7 ingredients in saucepan, mixing well.
Cook .... over medium heat until bubbly, stirring frequently.
Spoon ...... into 9 x 13-inch baking dish.
Cover ...... with sheets of crescent roll dough.
Mix .... remaining ingredients in bowl.
Spread ..... over dough.
Bake .... at 375 degrees for 25 minutes or until golden brown.
Yields ...... 6-8 servings.

Vera M. Shannon
Laureate Xi, Springfield, Missouri

CURRIED TURKEY CASSEROLE

2 lg. packages frozen chopped broccoli, thawed, drained
8 c. chopped cooked turkey
1 can each cream of chicken, celery, mushroom soup
1 c. milk
1 c. mayonnaise
2 tsp. curry
1 tbsp. lemon juice
1 lb. mild Cheddar cheese, grated

Layer ...... broccoli and turkey in 2 buttered 11 x 13-inch baking pans.
Blend ...... remaining ingredients except cheese in bowl.
Pour .... over turkey.
Top .... with cheese.
Bake .... loosely covered, at 350 degrees for 45 to 60 minutes or until bubbly.
Yields ...... 20-25 servings.

Joan L. Eshelman
Theta Tau, Meeker, Colorado

TURKEY INDIENNE

1/2 c. chopped green pepper
2 tbsp. shortening
2 c. flour
1 can mushroom soup
1/2 tsp. curry
2 tbsp. dry onion soup mix
2 c. chopped cooked turkey
1/4 c. chopped almonds
Bean sprouts (opt.)

Saute ...... green pepper in shortening in skillet until tender.
Blend ...... flour with 1/2 cup water in bowl.
Stir .... into green pepper with next 3 ingredients.
Cook .... until thick, stirring constantly.
Add .... turkey, almonds and bean sprouts, mixing well.
Simmer ..... for 10 minutes.
Serve .... over rice.
Yields ...... 4-6 servings.

Eileen R. Brereton
Laureate Alpha, Salt Lake City, Utah

TURKEY ORIENTAL

1 c. sliced celery
1 6-oz. package frozen pea pods
1 green pepper, cut into strips
1 tbsp. margarine
1 pkg. onion gravy mix
1/4 tsp. cinnamon
2 tsp. soy sauce
3 pimentos, sliced
8 oz. water chestnuts, sliced
2 c. slivered cooked turkey
2 c. cooked rice

Saute ...... first 3 ingredients in margarine in skillet until tender-crisp.
Stir .... in gravy mix, cinnamon, soy sauce and 1 cup water.
Bring .... to a boil; reduce heat.
Add .... next 3 ingredients, mixing well.
Layer ...... rice and turkey mixture in 2-quart casserole.
Bake .... at 350 degrees for 30 minutes.
Yields ...... 6 servings.

Lachelle Boettcher
Alpha Epsilon, Rock Springs, Wyoming

Seafood

HOT CRAB-AVOCADO CASSEROLES

1/4 c. butter, melted
3 tbsp. flour
1 tsp. salt
1/4 tsp. each red pepper, thyme
2 c. milk
2 avocados
Lemon juice
2 7 1/2-oz. cans crab meat, drained, flaked
2 tbsp. Le Blanc de Blancs
1/2 c. Parmesan cheese

Blend ...... butter, flour and seasonings in saucepan.
Stir .... in milk gradually.
Cook .... until thick, stirring constantly.
Chop .... avocados, reserving 4 lengthwise slices for garnish.
Coat .... with lemon juice.
Add .... crab meat, wine and avocado, mixing well.
Spoon ...... into 4 small casseroles.
Sprinkle .... with cheese.
Broil .... for 2 minutes or until golden.
Garnish ..... with avocado slices.
Yields ...... 4 servings.

Photograph for this recipe on page 77.

IMPERIAL CREAMED CRAB MEAT

1 lb. cooked crab meat, flaked
2 tbsp. lemon juice
4 oz. cream cheese, softened
1/2 c. cream
3 green onions, finely chopped
1/4 tsp. dillweed
Salt and pepper to taste
6 scallop shells (opt.)
1/4 c. Parmesan cheese
1/4 c. bread crumbs
2 tbsp. melted butter

Combine .... first 8 ingredients in bowl, blending well.
Spoon ...... into shells.
Mix .... cheese, bread crumbs and butter in bowl.
Sprinkle .... over shells.
Bake .... at 350 degrees for 15 minutes or until heated through.

Diki Engberg
Preceptor Laureate Alpha, Salt Lake City, Utah

TASTY CRAB CASSEROLE

4 slices bread, cubed
1/2 lb. sharp Cheddar cheese, grated
1/2 green pepper, chopped
1 med. onion, chopped
1/2 c. chopped celery
Butter
1 egg
1 can shrimp, drained
1 can crab meat, drained
1/2 c. mayonnaise
Tabasco sauce to taste
Ritz cracker crumbs

Combine .... bread and cheese with 1 cup water in large bowl.
Saute ...... green pepper, onion and celery in butter in skillet.
Stir .... into bread and cheese mixture.
Beat .... in egg.
Add .... next 4 ingredients, mixing well.
Spoon ...... into greased 3-quart casserole.
Top .... with Ritz cracker crumbs.
Dot .... with butter.
Bake .... at 400 degrees for 30 minutes or until heated through.

Sherry Sugg
Alpha Theta Phi, Edinburg, Texas

LOBSTER AND MUSHROOM CASSEROLE

1 lb. mushrooms, sliced
4 tbsp. butter
3 tbsp. flour
1 tsp. salt
Dash of pepper
1 1/2 c. milk
1/2 c. chicken broth
2 c. chopped lobster
2 egg yolks
1/2 c. cream
Bread crumbs

Saute ...... mushrooms in butter in saucepan for 5 minutes.
Add .... next 3 ingredients, mixing well.
Stir .... in milk and broth gradually.
Cook .... until thick, stirring constantly.
Add .... lobster, mixing well.
Beat .... egg yolks with cream in bowl.
Stir .... into lobster mixture.

Cook . . . . . . over low heat until heated through, stirring frequently.
Pour . . . . into buttered casserole.
Sprinkle . . . . with bread crumbs.
Bake . . . . at 450 degrees for 10 minutes.

Wanda Barkhurst
Preceptor Rho, Weirton, West Virginia

DIANE'S SCALLOP CASSEROLE

2 lb. scallops
1 egg yolk, beaten
1/2 c. light cream
1/4 c. white wine
2 tsp. lemon juice
1 tbsp. minced onion
1/8 tsp. each white pepper, ginger
1 1/2 tsp. salt
1 c. soft bread crumbs
2 tbsp. Parmesan cheese
2 tbsp. melted butter

Arrange . . . . . scallops over bottom of 2-quart casserole.
Combine . . . . next 5 ingredients with seasonings in bowl, mixing well.
Pour . . . . over scallops.
Toss . . . . bread crumbs with Parmesan cheese and butter in bowl.
Sprinkle . . . . over casserole.
Bake . . . . at 350 degrees for 30 minutes.
Bake . . . . at 450 degrees for 5 minutes longer or until brown.
Yields . . . . . . 6 servings.

Diane I. Wakeling
Theta Kappa, Aurora, Ontario, Canada

NORMA'S SCALLOP CASSEROLE

1 clove of garlic
1/2 c. butter, melted
1/2 c. minced onion
2 1/2 lb. scallops
1/4 c. dry white wine
2 tbsp. flour
1 c. half and half
Salt and white pepper to taste
1/2 c. cracker crumbs
1/4 c. Parmesan cheese

Saute . . . . . . garlic in 1/4 cup butter in saucepan for 2 minutes; remove garlic.

Add . . . . onion and scallops.
Saute . . . . . . for 3 minutes.
Stir . . . . in wine.
Cook . . . . for 3 minutes longer; remove scallops.
Blend . . . . . . flour into pan drippings.
Stir . . . . in half and half.
Cook . . . . over low heat for 2 minutes, stirring constantly.
Add . . . . seasonings.
Toss . . . . cracker crumbs with cheese and remaining 1/4 cup butter in bowl.
Layer . . . . . . scallops, sauce and cracker crumb mixture in buttered casserole.
Bake . . . . at 400 degrees for 15 minutes.
Garnish . . . . . with parsley.
Yields . . . . . . 8 servings.

Norma Swan
Alpha Delta, McAdam, New Brunswick, Canada

MARLENE'S SHRIMP CASSEROLE

1 green pepper, chopped
1 1/2 c. chopped onion
2 stalks celery, chopped
1 stick margarine, melted
3 c. shrimp
Salt and pepper to taste
1 can Ro-Tel
1 can cream of mushroom soup
2 c. cooked rice
1/4 c. chopped parsley
Bread crumbs

Saute . . . . . . green pepper, onion and celery in margarine in large saucepan.
Season . . . . . shrimp with salt and pepper.
Add . . . . shrimp and Ro-Tel to sauteed vegetables, mixing well.
Cook . . . . for 5 minutes.
Stir . . . . in soup.
Cook . . . . for 5 minutes longer.
Add . . . . rice and parsley, mixing well.
Spoon . . . . . . into greased 9 x 13-inch casserole.
Top . . . . with bread crumbs.
Bake . . . . at 450 degrees for 30 minutes.
Yields . . . . . . 6 servings.

Marlene L. Roy
Kappa, New Iberia, Louisiana

BAKED SHRIMP-CHEESE PUFF

4 slices buttered bread, cut into
*   1/2-in. cubes*
1/2 lb. shrimp, cut into bite-sized pieces
1/2 lb. cheese, grated
3 eggs, beaten
2 c. milk
1/4 tsp. dry mustard
Salt and pepper to taste

Layer . . . . . . bread, shrimp and cheese alternately in buttered 1 1/2-quart casserole.
Combine . . . . eggs, milk and seasonings in bowl, beating well.
Pour . . . . over casserole.
Top . . . . with additional cheese.
Bake . . . . at 350 degrees for 40 to 50 minutes or until puffed.
Yields . . . . . . 4-5 servings.

Marjorie E. Towslee
Preceptor Rho, Cartersville, Georgia

GOLDEN SHRIMP CASSEROLE

9 slices dried bread, trimmed, cubed
2 c. grated sharp Cheddar cheese
1 1/2 lb. cooked med. shrimp, cut into
*   bite-sized pieces*
1 3-oz. can sliced mushrooms
4 eggs
2 3/4 c. milk
3/4 tsp. dry mustard
1/2 tsp. salt
1 can frozen cream of shrimp soup, thawed

Place . . . . bread cubes in bottom of buttered 9 x 13-inch casserole.
Sprinkle . . . . cheese over top.
Layer . . . . . . shrimp and mushrooms over cheese.
Beat . . . . eggs, 2 1/4 cups milk, dry mustard and salt in bowl until well blended.
Pour . . . . over mushrooms.
Chill . . . . covered, overnight.
Blend . . . . . . soup and 1/2 cup milk in bowl.
Pour . . . . over casserole.
Bake . . . . at 300 degrees for 1 1/2 hours.
Yields . . . . . . 8 servings.

Marilyn Slaughter
Xi Delta, Kingsport, Tennessee

SHRIMP-RICE CASSEROLE

1 8-oz. package frozen shrimp, cooked
2 c. cooked rice
3 tbsp. minced onion
1 8-oz. can tiny green peas
Salt and pepper to taste
1 1/2 tsp. Worcestershire sauce
1 pkg. dry onion soup mix
1 c. mayonnaise
1 c. Pepperidge Farm stuffing mix
Butter

Combine . . . . first 9 ingredients in 2-quart casserole.
Sprinkle . . . . with stuffing mix.
Dot . . . . with butter.
Bake . . . . at 350 degrees for 30 minutes.
Yields . . . . . . 6-8 servings.

Peggy May and Eleanor Brooks
Xi Alpha Theta, Burlington, North Carolina

SHRIMP AND ASPARAGUS CASSEROLE

12 asparagus spears, cooked
1/2 lb. mushrooms, sliced
4 tbsp. butter, melted
2 tbsp. flour
1 c. milk
2 tbsp. Sherry
1 c. grated Swiss cheese
Dash each of pepper, nutmeg
1 lb. cooked shrimp
1/2 c. dry bread crumbs

Arrange . . . . . asparagus over bottom of 8 x 12-inch casserole.
Saute . . . . . . mushrooms in butter in saucepan.
Blend . . . . . . in flour.
Stir . . . . in milk and Sherry gradually.
Cook . . . . until thick, stirring constantly.
Stir . . . . in 1/2 cup cheese, seasonings and shrimp.
Spoon . . . . . . over asparagus.
Top . . . . with bread crumbs and remaining 1/2 cup cheese.
Bake . . . . at 350 degrees for 20 minutes or until golden brown.
Yields . . . . . . 6-8 servings.

Kelly Smith
Laureate Gamma, Eagle River, Alaska

MONROEVILLE'S FAVORITE SHRIMP CASSEROLE

1 lb. boiled shrimp
2 cans cream of mushroom soup
1 c. mayonnaise
2 pimentos finely chopped
1 clove of garlic, minced
2 tsp. Worcestershire sauce
Salt and pepper to taste
2 hard-boiled eggs, sliced
1/2 c. bread crumbs
1/2 c. slivered almonds

Combine . . . . all ingredients except crumbs and almonds in bowl, mixing well.
Spoon . . . . . . into greased 3-quart casserole.
Toss . . . . bread crumbs with almonds.
Sprinkle . . . . over casserole.
Bake . . . . at 350 degrees for 20 minutes.
Yields . . . . . . 8 servings.

Eugenie S. Crandall
Epsilon Phi, Monroeville, Alabama

SHRIMP AND MUSHROOM CASSEROLE

1 lb. cooked shrimp
1/4 c. melted butter
1 1/2 c. grated American cheese
3 tbsp. chili sauce
1/2 tsp. Worcestershire sauce
1/2 tsp. salt
Dash of pepper
2 tbsp. chopped pimento
1   3-oz. can sliced mushrooms
1/2 c. heavy cream
1 1/2 c. cooked rice
1/2 c. corn chips, crushed

Combine . . . . all ingredients except rice and corn chips in bowl, mixing well.
Layer . . . . . . rice and shrimp mixture alternately in 1 1/2-quart casserole until all ingredients are used ending with shrimp mixture.
Top . . . . with corn chips.
Bake . . . . at 350 degrees for 25 minutes.
Yields . . . . . . 6 servings.

Emily K. Mason
Beta Theta, Laurel, Maryland

COMPANY SHRIMP CASSEROLE

1/2 c. each chopped green pepper,
   green onion, celery
1 stick butter
2 to 3 lb. shrimp, cooked
1 c. rice, cooked
1 c. sharp cheese, grated
1 can mushroom soup
2 lg. lemons, thinly sliced

Saute . . . . . . green pepper, onion and celery in butter in skillet until tender.
Combine . . . . with shrimp, rice, cheese and soup in large bowl, mixing well.
Spoon . . . . . . into 9 x 13-inch baking dish.
Cover . . . . . . with lemon slices.
Bake . . . . covered, at 375 degrees for 20 minutes or until heated through.
Yields . . . . . . 6 servings.

Barbara Bain
Preceptor Beta Psi, Beaumont, Texas

SEAFOOD STUFFING SUPREME

1/2 c. each chopped celery, onion
2 tbsp. butter
1 can cream of shrimp soup
1/4 c. chopped parsley
1/4 c. milk
1/2 tsp. sage
1/4 tsp. thyme
Dash of pepper
2 eggs, beaten
4 c. dry French bread cubes
1 or 2   4 1/2-oz. cans shrimp, drained

Saute . . . . . . celery and onion in butter in 3-quart saucepan until tender.
Stir . . . . in soup, parsley, milk, sage, thyme and pepper.
Add . . . . eggs, bread and shrimp, mixing well.
Spoon . . . . . . into 1 1/2-quart casserole.
Bake . . . . covered, at 350 degrees for 30 minutes.
Bake . . . . uncovered, for 10 minutes longer.
Garnish . . . . . with additional shrimp and parsley.
Yields . . . . . . 5 servings.

Anne F. Beirth
Laureate Rho, Norristown, Pennsylvania

LIZ'S SHRIMP DIVAN

1 med. onion, finely chopped
1/2 c. finely chopped green pepper
1 sm. apple, chopped
1 tbsp. curry powder
1 tsp. salt
3 tbsp. butter, melted
3 tbsp. flour
2 c. milk
1/4 c. lemon juice
1 can Cheddar cheese soup
3 c. cooked egg noodles
1 lg. bag frozen broccoli, thawed
12 slices cooked chicken
1 lb. small shrimp, cooked

Saute ...... onion, green pepper, apple and seasonings in butter in skillet until onion is tender.
Stir .... in flour.
Mix .... milk, lemon juice and soup in bowl.
Stir .... into onion mixture gradually.
Cook ...... until heated through, stirring frequently.
Layer ...... noodles, broccoli, chicken, shrimp and soup mixture in 9 x 13-inch baking dish.
Sprinkle .... with paprika.
Bake .... at 350 degrees for 1 hour.
Yields ...... 6-8 servings.

Elizabeth K. Jackson
Xi Alpha, Mililani, Hawaii

FAVORITE SHRIMP CASSEROLE

1 each med. onion, green pepper, chopped
3 stalks celery, chopped
1 stick butter
2 to 3 lb. shrimp, cut into bite-sized pieces
Salt, pepper and garlic powder to taste
1 c. rice
1 can cream of mushroom soup
1 can Ro-Tel
1/4 c. chopped parsley (opt.)

Saute ...... onion, green pepper and celery in butter in skillet until tender.
Season ..... shrimp with salt, pepper and garlic powder.
Combine .... all ingredients in 9 x 12-inch baking dish, mixing well.

Bake .... at 350 degrees for 1 hour or until rice is tender.
Yields ...... 6-8 servings.

Merline McCoy
Preceptor Gamma Alpha, Port Neches, Texas

TEDO'S CREAMY SHRIMP AND NOODLES

1 c. finely chopped onion
1/2 c. finely chopped green pepper
1 c. chopped drained tomatoes
1 1/2 lb. shrimp
3 tbsp. melted margarine
1 tbsp. paprika
1 tsp. salt
1/4 tsp. pepper
1 c. sour cream
1 13-oz. package cream cheese, cubed
1 18-oz. package thin noodles, cooked, drained

Cook .... first 4 ingredients in margarine in large skillet over medium-low heat for 20 minutes, stirring occasionally.
Add .... seasonings, sour cream and cream cheese, mixing well.
Cook .... until cream cheese is melted, stirring constantly. Do not boil.
Stir .... in noodles.
Yields ...... 4 servings.

Betty A. Christianson
Preceptor Zeta, Great Falls, Montana

JAMBALAYA

1 lb. shrimp
3/4 c. melted butter
1 can Ro-Tel
1 lg. onion, chopped
1 green pepper, chopped
1 can onion soup with beef stock
1 can cream of chicken soup
2 c. rice

Combine .... all ingredients with 1 soup can water in bowl, mixing well.
Spoon ...... into 2 1/2-quart casserole.
Bake .... at 425 degrees for 1 1/2 hours.
Yields ...... 8 servings.

Maggie Hildebrand
Alpha Theta Zeta, Houston, Texas

SHRIMP DELIGHT

1 green pepper, chopped
1 onion, chopped
1 stick margarine
2 c. rice
1 can each onion, cream of celery soup
1 1/2 lb. shrimp

Saute ...... green pepper and onion in margarine in skillet until tender.
Stir .... in rice and soups.
Add .... shrimp, mixing well.
Spoon ...... into greased 9 x 13-inch casserole.
Bake .... covered, at 350 degrees for 30 minutes; stir.
Bake .... covered, for 30 minutes longer.
Yields ...... 6-8 servings.

Kay Shaver
Alpha Xi Nu, Houston, Texas

DELICIOUS SHRIMP CASSEROLE

3 slices bread
Milk
1 c. each chopped onion, celery, green pepper
4 cloves of garlic, minced
Butter
2 tbsp. chopped parsley
1/2 c. chopped green onion tops
1 c. white sauce
Pinch each of curry, seasoned salt
2 oz. white wine
3 c. cooked rice
1 c. chopped mushrooms
3 c. shrimp
Bread crumbs

Soak .... bread in milk in bowl.
Saute ...... onion, celery, green pepper and garlic in 1 stick butter in skillet.
Add .... bread, 1/4 cup hot water and next 9 ingredients, mixing well.
Cook .... for 8 minutes.
Spoon ...... into 2-quart casserole.
Top .... with bread crumbs.
Dot .... with butter.
Bake .... at 350 degrees for 30 minutes.
Yields ...... 6-8 servings.

Tommie Billingsley
Xi Beta Eta, Horseshoe Bend, Arkansas

SHRIMP ROYAL

3 tbsp. minced onion
2 tbsp. melted butter
1 lb. shrimp
1/4 lb. mushrooms
3 tbsp. chili sauce
Salt and pepper to taste
1 1/3 c. minute rice
1 c. sour cream
1 tbsp. flour

Saute ...... onion in butter in skillet until lightly browned.
Add .... shrimp and mushrooms.
Cook .... until shrimp are lightly browned, stirring frequently.
Combine .... chili sauce, salt and pepper with 1 2/3 cups water in bowl, mixing well.
Add .... to shrimp mixture, mixing well.
Bring .... to a boil.
Stir .... in rice.
Simmer ..... covered, for 5 minutes.
Blend ...... sour cream and flour in bowl.
Add .... to shrimp mixture, mixing well.
Cook .... until heated through.
Yields ...... 8 servings.

Opal G. Cressy
Xi Pi Lambda, Desert Shores, California

EASY SHRIMP AND WILD RICE

1 sm. onion, chopped
1/2 c. chopped celery
1/2 green pepper, chopped
1 sm. can mushrooms
1/4 c. butter
2 c. shrimp, cooked
1 can cream of mushroom soup
1/4 c. milk
1/2 c. wild rice, cooked

Saute ...... onion, celery, green pepper and mushrooms in butter in skillet for 5 minutes.
Add .... remaining 4 ingredients, mixing well.
Spoon ...... into greased 2-quart casserole.
Bake .... at 350 degrees for 45 minutes.
Yields ...... 6 servings.

Sharon L. Lundeen
Xi Gamma Omicron, Marshall, Missouri

SORORITY'S FAVORITE SEAFOOD CASSEROLE

1   1-lb. can crab meat
1 lb. shrimp, cooked
1 c. mayonnaise
1/2 c. chopped green pepper
1/4 c. finely chopped onion
1 1/2 c. finely chopped celery
1/2 tsp. salt
1 tbsp. Worcestershire sauce
2 c. coarsely crushed potato chips
Paprika

Combine .... first 8 ingredients in bowl, mixing well.
Spoon ...... into buttered 2 1/2-quart casserole.
Top .... with potato chips.
Sprinkle .... with paprika.
Bake .... at 400 degrees for 20 to 25 minutes or until heated through.
Yields ...... 8 servings.

Margaret W. McGinnis
Xi Delta Epsilon, Flemingsburg, Kentucky

CRAB AND SHRIMP ELEGANTE

1/2 lb. each crab meat, shrimp
1 lg. can artichoke hearts, drained,
   cut into halves
3 green onion tops, chopped
1 tbsp. Worcestershire sauce
Dash of Tabasco sauce
2 cans cream of mushroom soup
1/2 c. Parmesan cheese

Combine.... first 7 ingredients and 1/4 cup Parmesan cheese in bowl, mixing well.
Spoon ...... into greased casserole.
Top .... with remaining 1/4 cup Parmesan cheese.
Bake .... at 350 degrees for 20 to 30 minutes or until bubbly.
Yields ...... 6 servings.

Chere Duffy
Delta Zeta Chi, Danville, California

LONG BEACH SEAFOOD

2 cans frozen shrimp soup
2 tbsp. Sherry

2 sm. cans button mushrooms, drained
Almonds (opt.)
1/2 lb. crab meat
1/2 lb. small shrimp
Cheddar cheese, sliced
Paprika

Combine .... first 4 ingredients in 2-quart casserole, mixing well.
Fold .... in seafood.
Cover ...... with cheese.
Sprinkle .... with paprika.
Chill .... for several hours.
Bake .... at 300 degrees for 1 hour.
Serve .... in patty shells.
Yields ...... 4-6 servings.

Natalie E. Steed
Preceptor Laureate Phi, San Diego, California

CRAB AND SHRIMP-STUFFED SHELLS

18 to 20 lg. shell macaroni
2 pkg. frozen chopped spinach, cooked,
   well drained
2   7 1/2-oz. cans sm. shrimp
2   7 1/2-oz. cans crab meat
2 1/2 tbsp. mayonnaise
1/4 c. Italian bread crumbs
8 oz. Cheddar cheese, shredded
2 cans cream of shrimp soup

Cook .... macaroni in water in saucepan until just tender; drain.
Spread ..... spinach over bottom of greased 8 x 10-inch casserole.
Combine .... shrimp, crab meat, mayonnaise and bread crumbs in bowl, mixing well.
Stuff .... shells with mixture.
Place .... over spinach.
Sprinkle .... with cheese.
Top .... with soup.
Bake .... at 350 degrees for 25 to 30 minutes or until bubbly.
Yields ...... 4-6 servings.

Carol Carroll
Xi Chi, Winchester, Virginia

EASY SEAFOOD CASSEROLE

1 can sm. shrimp, drained
1 can crab meat, flaked

1 c. each chopped celery, onion
1 c. minced green pepper
1 c. mayonnaise
Salt and pepper to taste
1 tbsp. Worcestershire sauce
1/2 c. milk
1 c. buttered herb stuffing mix

Combine .... first 10 ingredients with 3/4 cup stuffing mix in bowl, mixing well.
Spoon ...... into buttered baking dish.
Top .... with remaining 1/4 cup stuffing mix.
Bake .... at 350 degrees for 30 minutes.
Yields ...... 8 servings.

Kay Moore
Preceptor Rho, Waterloo, Iowa

SEAFOOD DELIGHT

1 lb. crab meat
1 lb. cooked shrimp
1 lb. lobster
2 c. mayonnaise
1/4 c. chopped onion
1/2 c. chopped green pepper
1 1/2 c. chopped celery
1/2 tsp. salt
1 tbsp. Worcestershire sauce
2 c. crushed potato chips
Paprika

Combine .... first 9 ingredients in bowl, mixing well.
Spoon ...... into buttered 3-quart casserole.
Top .... with potato chips.
Sprinkle .... with paprika.
Bake .... at 400 degrees for 20 to 25 minutes or until bubbly.
Serve .... over rice.
Yields ...... 12 servings.

Bettie Lou Plummer
Laureate Pi, Independence, Missouri

SEAFOOD NOODLE BAKE

2 c. chopped onion
1/2 c. butter, melted
2 cans cream of mushroom soup
2 cans cream of shrimp soup

2 c. milk
2 c. shredded Cheddar cheese
3 7 1/2-oz. cans crab meat, drained, flaked
3 4 1/2-oz. cans shrimp, drained
2 6-oz. cans sliced mushrooms
1/3 c. chopped parsley
16 oz. noodles, cooked, drained
3 c. soft bread crumbs

Cook .... onion in 6 tablespoons butter in large saucepan until tender, stirring often.
Stir .... in soups and milk.
Cook ...... until smooth, stirring constantly.
Add .... cheese, mixing well.
Cook .... until cheese is melted, stirring constantly; remove from heat.
Stir .... in crab meat, shrimp, mushrooms and parsley.
Place .... noodles in two 9 x 13-inch baking pans.
Spoon ...... crab meat mixture into pans, mixing gently.
Toss .... bread crumbs with remaining 2 tablespoons butter.
Sprinkle .... over top.
Bake .... at 350 degrees for 35 to 45 minutes or until bubbly.
Yields ...... 24 servings.

Melinda Jenkins
Xi Zeta, Sitka, Alaska

MORRIS' SEAFOOD CASSEROLE

1 can cream of shrimp soup
2 c. white sauce
1/2 can Cheddar cheese soup
1 can mushrooms
3 oz. white wine
1 1/2 lb. fish fillets, baked, flaked
Crushed corn flakes

Combine .... first 5 ingredients in saucepan, mixing well.
Simmer ..... for several minutes.
Add .... fish, mixing well.
Pour .... into 9 x 9-inch baking dish.
Top .... with corn flakes.
Bake .... at 350 degrees for 20 minutes.
Yields ...... 6 servings.

Marsha K. Englebrick
Xi Rho Mu, San Jose, California

SALMON-DILL SALAD WITH PASTA SHELLS

1/4 lb. smoked salmon
1/4 c. mayonnaise
1/4 c. yogurt
3 tbsp. chopped shallots
Finely chopped fresh dill
Pepper to taste
1/2 lb. pasta shells, cooked, drained

Cut . . . . salmon into slivers.
Combine . . . . next 5 ingredients in bowl, mixing well.
Toss . . . . mixture with salmon and pasta shells.
Chill . . . . for several hours before serving.

Photograph for this recipe on page 89.

LAYERED SALMON BAKE

1 1/2 c. evaporated milk
2 eggs, slightly beaten
1 tbsp. lemon juice
1/2 tsp. salt
1/4 c. each chopped onion, green pepper
1/4 tsp. each pepper, dillweed, dry mustard
2 c. dry bread cubes
1 c. shredded Cheddar cheese
1 pkg. frozen chopped broccoli
1 c. drained canned corn
1   15-oz. can salmon, drained
1 c. dry bread cubes, crushed

Combine . . . . first 4 ingredients with onion, green pepper and seasonings in bowl, mixing well.
Layer . . . . . . bread cubes, cheese, broccoli, corn, salmon and evaporated milk mixture in greased 9-inch baking dish.
Sprinkle . . . . crushed bread cubes over top.
Chill . . . . covered, overnight.
Bake . . . . uncovered, at 350 degrees for 1 hour.

Patricia A. Brandt
Delta Xi, Oelwein, Iowa

PINK SALMON CASSEROLE

3 tbsp. flour
1/4 tsp. salt
1/8 tsp. pepper
1 tbsp. chopped chives
1/4 c. butter
2 c. milk
1 to 2 tsp. prepared mustard
1 tsp. grated lemon rind
2 tbsp. lemon juice
1   3 or 4-oz. can sliced mushrooms
1   10-oz. package frozen asparagus spears, cooked, drained
1 c. cooked noodles
1   7 3/4-oz. can pink salmon, drained. flaked
1/2 c. buttered corn flake crumbs

Blend . . . . . . flour, salt, pepper, chives and butter in saucepan.
Add . . . . milk gradually.
Cook . . . . until thick, stirring constantly.
Stir . . . . in mustard, lemon rind and juice and mushrooms.
Cut . . . . asparagus into 1-inch pieces, reserving several spears for garnish.
Add . . . . cut asparagus to white sauce with noodles and salmon, mixing well.
Spoon . . . . . . into greased 1 1/2-quart baking dish.
Top . . . . with buttered corn flake crumbs.
Bake . . . . at 350 degrees for 25 to 35 minutes.
Garnish . . . . . with reserved asparagus spears and lemon quarters.

Photograph for this recipe above.

FILLET OF SOLE CASSEROLE

1 1/2 lb. fillets of sole
2 oz. shredded Swiss cheese
1/4 c. chopped green onion
1 2-oz. can sliced mushrooms
1/2 can cream of shrimp soup
1/4 c. cream Sherry
1/2 tsp. prepared mustard
1 tsp. chopped parsley
Pinch each of cayenne pepper, nutmeg
Salt and pepper to taste
Paprika

Arrange . . . . . fillets over bottom of shallow 6 x 10-inch baking dish.
Sprinkle . . . . with cheese and onion.
Combine . . . . next 9 ingredients in saucepan, mixing well.
Cook . . . . . . until heated through, stirring constantly.
Pour . . . . over fillets.
Sprinkle . . . . with paprika.
Bake . . . . at 375 degrees for 15 to 20 minutes or until bubbly.
Yields . . . . . . 6 servings.

Nina K. Bunnell
Laureate Pi, Medford, Oregon

SOLE FLORENTINE

2 pkg. frozen spinach, thawed, well drained
1 lb. fillets of sole
2 tbsp. butter
3 tbsp. flour
1/2 tsp. salt
1/4 tsp. pepper
Pinch of nutmeg
1 1/2 c. milk
1 c. grated Cheddar cheese
Fine bread crumbs

Layer . . . . . . spinach and sole in 11 x 13-inch baking pan.
Melt . . . . butter in saucepan.
Stir . . . . in flour, salt, pepper and nutmeg.
Add . . . . milk, stirring until blended.
Cook . . . . over low heat until thick, stirring constantly.
Add . . . . cheese.
Cook . . . . until cheese melts, stirring constantly.

Pour . . . . over sole.
Sprinkle . . . . with bread crumbs.
Bake . . . . at 350 degrees for 30 minutes.
Yields . . . . . . 4 servings.

Cod may be substituted for sole.

Barbara Fitsell
Laureate Alpha Alpha, Kingston, Ontario, Canada

EVERY DAY TUNA CASSEROLE

1 8-oz. package twist macaroni, cooked
1/4 green pepper, chopped
1 can tomato soup
1/2 can evaporated milk
1 can light chunk tuna
8 oz. Cheddar cheese, grated

Mix . . . . first 5 ingredients and half the cheese with 1/2 milk can water in 2-quart casserole.
Sprinkle . . . . remaining cheese over top.
Bake . . . . at 350 degrees for 30 to 45 minutes or until bubbly.

Margaret Mickler
Xi Zeta Alpha, St. Augustine, Florida

TUNA-MUSHROOM CASSEROLE

1 can mushrooms
Milk
1 can tuna
1 can cream of celery soup
1 can chop suey vegetables with mushrooms, drained
1 pkg. chow mein noodles
1/2 c. dry bread crumbs
1/2 c. grated American cheese

Drain . . . . . . mushrooms, reserving liquid.
Add . . . . enough milk to reserved liquid to measure 1 cup.
Combine . . . . with remaining ingredients except bread crumbs and cheese in bowl, mixing well.
Spoon . . . . . . into 2-quart casserole.
Combine . . . . bread crumbs and cheese in bowl, tossing to mix.
Sprinkle . . . . over casserole.
Bake . . . . at 350 degrees for 30 minutes.
Yields . . . . . . 8-10 servings.

Sally Ottensmann
Beta Sigma Phi No. 10529, Cape Coral, Florida

SCREWY LOUIE

1 can each cream of mushroom, cream
of chicken soup
1/2 lb. sharp Cheddar cheese, grated
1 pkg. spiral noodles, cooked, drained
2 cans tuna, rinsed, drained
1 c. salad dressing
1 jar pimentos, chopped
1 can sliced mushrooms
1 lg. can asparagus, drained

Combine .... soups with half the cheese in
large saucepan, mixing well.
Cook .... over low heat until cheese is
melted, stirring constantly.
Add .... next 5 ingredients, mixing well.
Layer ...... half the soup mixture, asparagus
and remaining soup mixture in 9
x 13-inch baking dish.
Sprinkle .... remaining cheese over top.
Bake .... at 350 degrees for 30 to 40 min-
utes or until bubbly.
Yields ...... 8 servings.

Jeanne Ellsworth
Iota Tau, Rock Rapids, Iowa

PARTY TUNA BAKE

3/4 c. chopped green pepper
3 c. sliced celery
2 med. onions, chopped
1/4 c. butter
3 cans cream of mushroom soup
1 1/2 c. milk
3 c. process cheese, cubed
1 1/2 c. mayonnaise
24 oz. medium noodles, cooked, drained
3 9 1/4-oz. cans tuna
3/4 c. chopped pimento
1 c. slivered almonds

Saute ...... first 3 ingredients in butter in
skillet for 5 minutes.
Combine .... soup, milk and cheese in large
saucepan, mixing well.
Cook .... until cheese is melted, stirring
frequently.
Mix .... in mayonnaise.
Combine .... noodles, sauteed vegetables, tuna
and pimento in large bowl, mix-
ing well.
Stir .... in soup mixture.
Spoon ...... into 2 greased 9 x 13-inch
casseroles.

Sprinkle .... with almonds.
Bake .... at 400 degrees for 30 to 35 min-
utes or until bubbly.
Yields ...... 24 to 30 servings.

Virginia Ray
Preceptor Laureate Rho, Grandview, Missouri

FAVORITE TUNA CASSEROLE

1 8-oz. package egg noodles, cooked
2 sm. cans tuna, drained
1 can cream of mushroom soup
1 jar sliced mushrooms
1 med. onion, chopped
1 tsp. thyme
1/2 tsp. salt
1/4 tsp. (or more) pepper
1/2 c. sour cream
2 c. grated cheese
Bread crumbs (opt.)

Combine .... first 9 ingredients in bowl, mix-
ing well.
Spoon ...... into casserole.
Top .... with cheese and bread crumbs.
Bake .... at 350 degrees for 25 to 30 min-
utes or until bubbly.
Yields ...... 6-8 servings.

Rebecca G. Calhoun
Epsilon Mu, Mansfield, Louisiana

EASY TUNA CASSEROLE

1 lg. can tuna
1 c. cooked rice
1 sm. onion, minced
1 egg, beaten
1/2 tsp. salt
Juice of 1/2 lemon
1 c. chopped celery
1/2 c. chopped green pepper
1 can mushroom soup
1 c. Parmesan cheese

Combine .... all ingredients except Parmesan
cheese in bowl, mixing well.
Spoon ...... into greased baking dish.
Sprinkle .... Parmesan cheese over top.
Bake .... at 350 degrees for 30 to 40 min-
utes or until bubbly.
Yields ...... 4-6 servings.

Jane Marie Cervantes
Beta Lambda, Dayton, Ohio

Vegetables & Side Dishes

ASPARAGUS IN CHEESE SAUCE

2 cans asparagus tips, drained
1 can English peas, drained
3 tbsp. chopped pimento
3 hard-boiled eggs, sliced
1 c. grated sharp cheese
1 recipe med. white sauce
Sesame seed
Paprika

Layer ...... first 4 ingredients in order given in greased 9 x 13-inch casserole.
Combine .... cheese and white sauce in saucepan.
Cook .... over low heat until cheese melts, stirring constantly.
Pour .... over casserole.
Sprinkle .... with sesame seed and paprika.
Bake .... at 350 degrees for 30 minutes or until bubbly.
Yields ...... 8 servings.

Patsy M. Lynch
Xi Tau, Tuscaloosa, Alabama

EGG AND ASPARAGUS CASSEROLE

4 slices toasted white bread, cubed
6 tbsp. butter, melted
2 tbsp. flour
1 1/2 c. milk
1 tbsp. chopped parsley
1/4 tsp. pepper
3/4 tsp. salt
1/2 c. grated American cheese
12 oz. frozen asparagus tips, cooked, drained
4 hard-boiled eggs, sliced

Toss .... bread cubes with 2 tablespoons butter in bowl; set aside.
Blend ...... flour with 4 tablespoons butter in saucepan.
Stir .... in milk gradually until smooth.
Cook .... until thick, stirring constantly.
Add .... next 4 ingredients, mixing well.
Place .... half the bread cubes in greased baking dish.
Layer ...... asparagus and eggs alternately over bread cubes until all ingredients are used.
Pour .... cheese sauce over all.
Top .... with remaining bread cubes.

Bake .... at 350 degrees for 15 minutes or until bubbly.
Yields ...... 4 servings.

Esther L. Miller
Laureate Xi, Montrose, Colorado

GREEN BEAN PUFF

1   16-oz. can green beans
1 tbsp. finely chopped onion
2 tbsp. butter, melted
2 tbsp. flour
1/2 tsp. salt
1/8 tsp. marjoram
Dash of pepper
3/4 c. milk
2 eggs, separated
1/2 c. shredded sharp Cheddar cheese

Drain ...... beans, reserving 1/4 cup liquid.
Place .... beans in round 8-inch baking dish.
Saute ...... onion in butter in saucepan until just tender.
Stir .... in flour, 1/4 teaspoon salt, marjoram and pepper.
Add .... milk and reserved bean liquid, mixing well.
Cook .... over medium heat until thick, stirring constantly.
Pour .... over beans.
Beat .... egg whites and 1/4 teaspoon salt in bowl until stiff peaks form.
Stir .... cheese into well-beaten egg yolks.
Fold .... into egg whites.
Spread ..... over bean mixture.
Bake .... at 375 degrees for 15 to 20 minutes.
Yields ...... 4 servings.

Vivian A. Martin
Delta Omega, Beaverton, Oregon

GREEN BEANS SUPREME

1 can bamboo shoots, drained
1 can water chestnuts, drained, chopped
1 sm. can mushrooms, drained, chopped
1 stick margarine
1 can French-style green beans, drained
1 can mushroom soup

Saute . . . . . . first 3 ingredients in margarine in skillet until tender.
Layer . . . . . . half the green beans and sauteed vegetables in buttered 2-quart casserole.
Repeat . . . . . layers with remaining ingredients.
Spread . . . . . soup over top.
Garnish . . . . with salted nuts and toasted bread crumbs.
Bake . . . . at 350 degrees for 25 to 30 minutes or until heated through.
Yields . . . . . . 6 servings.

Mary Pinckard
Alpha Pi, DeFuniak Springs, Florida

SWISS-STYLE GREEN BEANS

2 c. green beans
1/2 lb. Swiss cheese, grated
2 tbsp. flour
1/4 c. butter, melted
1/2 tsp. onion flakes
1 tsp. each salt, sugar
1/4 tsp. pepper
1 c. sour cream
1 c. corn flakes, crushed

Combine . . . . green beans and cheese in greased casserole, mixing well.
Blend . . . . . . flour with 2 tablespoons butter in saucepan.
Stir . . . . in next 5 ingredients.
Cook . . . . over low heat until heated through, stirring constantly.
Pour . . . . over green bean mixture.
Toss . . . . corn flakes with remaining 2 tablespoons butter in bowl.
Sprinkle . . . . over top.
Bake . . . . at 350 degrees for 30 minutes.
Yields . . . . . . 10 servings.

Jean Barton
Preceptor Eta Gamma, Auburn, California

WESTERN LIMA BAKE

1 lb. dried lima beans
Salt to taste
1/2 lb. hamburger
1 onion, chopped
Pepper to taste
2 cans tomato sauce

Cook . . . . beans in salted water in saucepan until tender; drain, reserving 1/2 cup liquid.
Brown . . . . . . hamburger with onion, salt and pepper in skillet, stirring until crumbly.
Stir . . . . in tomato sauce, reserved liquid and beans.
Place . . . . in casserole.
Bake . . . . covered, at 350 degrees for 1 hour.
Yields . . . . . . 5-6 servings.

Carol Boss
Preceptor Theta Gamma, Mt. Shasta, California

BROCCOLI-PECAN CASSEROLE

2 10-oz. packages frozen broccoli, cooked, drained
1 pkg. dry onion soup mix
1 stick butter, melted
1 can sliced water chestnuts
1 c. chopped pecans
Buttered bread crumbs

Mix . . . . first 5 ingredients in casserole.
Top . . . . with bread crumbs.
Bake . . . . at 350 degrees for 25 minutes.

Margo Shriver
Xi Epsilon Sigma, Sanford, Florida

GREEN AND BROWN

1 10-oz. package frozen chopped broccoli, thawed, drained
4 lg. eggs, beaten
2 c. milk
2 c. cooked brown rice
1 1/2 c. coarsely grated Cheddar cheese
1/2 to 1 4-oz. can chopped green chilies, drained
1/2 tsp. salt

Combine . . . . all ingredients in large bowl, mixing well.
Spoon . . . . . . into 2-quart baking dish.
Bake . . . . at 350 degrees for 40 minutes or until knife inserted in center comes out clean.
Let . . . . stand for 10 minutes before serving.

Clara Lundgaard
Xi Upsilon Beta, Mineola, Texas

ROSE MARY'S BROCCOLI CHEESE STRATA

4 potatoes, thinly sliced
6 tbsp. butter, melted
1 1/2 tsp. salt
1/4 tsp. paprika
1/2 tsp. pepper
2 tbsp. flour
1 1/4 tbsp. milk
1/4 c. chopped pimento
1 c. shredded Cheddar cheese
1 10-oz. package frozen broccoli
   spears, thawed

Arrange . . . . . potato slices in greased 9 x 13-inch casserole.
Combine . . . . 4 tablespoons butter, 1 teaspoon salt, paprika and 1/4 teaspoon pepper in bowl, mixing well.
Brush . . . . . . potato slices with butter mixture.
Bake . . . . at 425 degrees for 45 minutes or until tender.
Combine . . . . remaining 2 tablespoons butter and flour in saucepan, stirring until well blended.
Stir . . . . in milk.
Cook . . . . over low heat until thick, stirring constantly.
Stir . . . . in remaining 1/2 teaspoon salt, 1/4 teaspoon pepper, pimento and Cheddar cheese.
Cook . . . . until cheese is melted, stirring frequently.
Arrange . . . . . broccoli over potatoes.
Pour . . . . cheese sauce over all.
Bake . . . . covered, for 10 minutes longer or until broccoli is tender.
Yields . . . . . . 4-6 servings.

Rose Mary Wells
Xi Upsilon Zeta, Corpus Christi, Texas

LORENE'S CABBAGE CASSEROLE

1 med. onion, chopped
3 tbsp. butter
1/2 lb. ground beef
3/4 tsp. salt
1/8 tsp. pepper
6 c. shredded cabbage
1 can tomato soup

Saute . . . . . . onion in butter in skillet.
Add . . . . ground beef, salt and pepper.

Cook . . . . . . until heated through. Do not brown.
Layer . . . . . . 3 cups cabbage and ground beef mixture in bottom of 2-quart baking dish.
Top . . . . with remaining 3 cups cabbage.
Pour . . . . soup over all.
Bake . . . . covered, at 350 degrees for 1 hour.
Yields . . . . . . 6 servings.

Lorene Hays
Laureate Beta, Longview, Washington

RED CABBAGE CASSEROLE

2 strips bacon, chopped
1 onion, finely chopped
2 tart apples, peeled, sliced
1 c. dry white wine
2 lb. red cabbage, cored, shredded
Salt and pepper to taste
1 tbsp. brown sugar
1 tbsp. vinegar

Brown . . . . . . bacon in saucepan until crisp.
Add . . . . onion and apples.
Cook . . . . until tender-crisp.
Add . . . . wine.
Bring . . . . . . to a boil.
Add . . . . remaining 5 ingredients, mixing well.
Spoon . . . . . . into 1 1/2-quart casserole.
Bake . . . . covered, at 350 degrees for 1 1/2 hours or until tender.
Yields . . . . . . 6-8 servings.

Patricia A. Webb
Xi Beta Chi, Metropolis, Illinois

CARROT CREATION

4 c. 1-inch carrot chunks
1 c. 1-inch potato chunks
6 tbsp. butter, melted
1 env. instant chicken bouillon
1/2 tsp. salt
1/2 c. fine soft bread crumbs

Cook . . . . carrots and potatoes in a small amount of water in covered saucepan until tender; drain, reserving 1/2 cup liquid.
Place . . . . half the vegetables and reserved liquid in blender container.
Puree . . . . . . for 3 minutes.

Add . . . . remaining vegetables.
Puree . . . . . . for 3 minutes longer.
Mix . . . . in 1/4 cup butter, bouillon and
salt.
Pour . . . . into shallow 1 1/2-quart baking
dish.
Toss . . . . bread crumbs with 2 tablespoons
butter in bowl.
Sprinkle . . . . over casserole.
Bake . . . . at 350 degrees for 25 to 30 min-
utes or until bubbly.
Yields . . . . . . 6 servings.

Betty M. Larkworthy
Laureate Upsilon, Stratford, Ontario, Canada

SAUCY CARROT CASSEROLE

1/2 lb. Velveeta cheese, cubed
1/2 stick butter
8 oz. sour cream
1 bunch green onions, chopped
2 lb. carrots, sliced
2 chicken bouillon cubes
Salt
Cracker crumbs

Melt . . . . cheese and butter in medium
saucepan, blending well.
Stir . . . . in sour cream and green onions.
Cook . . . . carrots with bouillon cubes in
salted water to cover in saucepan
until tender; drain.
Place . . . . in shallow 2-quart casserole.
Pour . . . . cheese mixture over carrots.
Top . . . . with cracker crumbs.
Bake . . . . at 350 degrees for 20 minutes.
Yields . . . . . . 6-8 servings.

Deborah J. Sanderson
Epsilon Omega, Sylva, North Carolina

COMPANY CELERY CASSEROLE

2 c. sliced celery
2 tbsp. butter, melted
1 can chicken with rice soup
1/4 c. buttered bread crumbs
1/4 c. slivered almonds

Cook . . . . celery in butter and 1/2 cup
water in saucepan until tender-
crisp.
Stir . . . . in soup.
Spoon . . . . . . into 1 1/2-quart casserole.

Top . . . . with crumbs and almonds.
Bake . . . . at 350 degrees for 20 minutes.
Yields . . . . . . 6 servings.

Alice D. Lauper
Preceptor Delta, Torrington, Connecticut

CHILES RELLENOS CASSEROLE

1 lg. can chilies, split, seeded
3/4 lb. Cheddar cheese, shredded
3/4 lb. Monterey Jack cheese, shredded
2 eggs, beaten
1 1/2 tbsp. flour
1 sm. can evaporated milk
1 6-oz. can tomato sauce

Layer . . . . . . first 3 ingredients alternately in
10-inch square baking dish.
Combine . . . . eggs, flour and milk in bowl,
mixing well.
Pour . . . . over layers.
Bake . . . . at 350 degrees for 30 minutes.
Top . . . . with tomato sauce.
Bake . . . . for 15 minutes longer.
Yields . . . . . . 6 servings.

Joyce Moro
Gamma Rho, Lakeside, Arizona

GULLINER'S CREAMED CORN

4 c. frozen corn
1 c. whipping cream
1 tsp. salt
1/2 tsp. each sugar, MSG
Butter
2 tsp. flour
Parmesan cheese

Cook . . . . corn in cream in saucepan until
heated through.
Stir . . . . in salt, sugar and MSG.
Melt . . . . 2 teaspoons butter in small
saucepan.
Add . . . . flour, mixing well.
Stir . . . . into corn mixture.
Cook . . . . until slightly thick, stirring
frequently.
Spoon . . . . . . into casserole.
Sprinkle . . . . Parmesan cheese over top.
Dot . . . . with butter.
Bake . . . . at 350 degrees for 25 minutes.
Yields . . . . . . 8-10 servings.

Verda Alfson
Preceptor Laureate Alpha, Williston, North Dakota

CORN PUDDING

1 can cream-style corn
1/2 tsp. salt
3 eggs, slightly beaten
1/4 tsp. each pepper, dry mustard
1 c. coarse cracker crumbs
1 c. milk
1 tsp. grated onion
1/2 c. chopped green pepper
1 2-oz. jar pimento strips
1/4 c. butter

Combine . . . . all ingredients except butter in bowl, mixing well.
Spoon . . . . . . into greased casserole.
Dot . . . . with butter.
Bake . . . . at 350 degrees for 1 hour or until set.
Yields . . . . . . 6 servings.

Jeannette Bradley
Exemplar Xi Psi, Brookfield, Missouri

EASY EGGPLANT CASSEROLE

1 med. eggplant, peeled, cut into
1-in. pieces
1/2 c. milk
1 egg, beaten
2 tbsp. butter, melted
1 sm. onion, chopped
1 c. seasoned bread crumbs
1/2 c. buttered bread crumbs

Cook . . . . eggplant in boiling salted water in saucepan for 8 minutes; drain.
Combine . . . . with next 5 ingredients in greased 2-quart baking dish, mixing well.
Top . . . . with buttered bread crumbs.
Bake . . . . at 350 degrees for 30 minutes.
Yields . . . . . . 4-5 servings.

Ellen B. Gates
Preceptor Laureate Eta, Carbondale, Illinois

EGGPLANT DRESSING

1 lg. eggplant, peeled, chopped
1/4 tsp. salt
1/2 c. chopped onion
1/2 c. chopped celery
2 c. corn bread crumbs
1 c. bread crumbs

1 can cream of chicken soup
2 tbsp. margarine
2 eggs
Salt and pepper to taste
1 c. grated cheese

Cook . . . . eggplant in salted water in saucepan until tender; drain.
Cook . . . . onion and celery in a small amount of water in saucepan until tender; drain.
Combine . . . . cooked vegetables and remaining ingredients except cheese in 2-quart casserole, mixing well.
Top . . . . with cheese.
Bake . . . . at 375 degrees for 20 minutes or until cheese is melted.
Yields . . . . . . 6 servings.

Marlene Baucum
Xi Xi, Phoenix, Arizona

FRESH MUSHROOM CASSEROLE

1 1/2 lb. fresh mushrooms, chopped
2 tbsp. butter
1/2 c. each chopped onion, celery,
green pepper
6 slices white bread, buttered, cubed
2 eggs, beaten
1 1/2 c. milk
1/2 c. mayonnaise
1 can cream of mushroom soup
1/2 c. Romano cheese
1 sm. can sliced ripe olives, drained

Saute . . . . . . mushrooms in butter in skillet until tender; drain.
Combine . . . . with onion, celery and green pepper in bowl, mixing well.
Place . . . . half the bread in greased casserole.
Top . . . . with vegetables and remaining bread.
Mix . . . . eggs, milk and mayonnaise in bowl.
Pour . . . . over casserole.
Chill . . . . for several hours.
Top . . . . with soup, cheese and olives.
Bake . . . . at 350 degrees for 1 hour.
Yields . . . . . . 6 servings.

Bernice Cogburn
Xi Eta Delta, Jacksonville, Florida

SCALLOPED MUSHROOMS

1 lb. mushrooms, sliced
1/4 lb. saltines, coarsely crushed
4 tbsp. melted margarine
1 c. whipping cream
Salt and paprika to taste
1 tbsp. margarine

Combine . . . . first 4 ingredients in bowl, mixing well.
Spoon . . . . . . into 2-quart casserole.
Sprinkle . . . . salt and paprika over top.
Dot . . . . with margarine.
Bake . . . . at 350 degrees for 45 minutes.

Rose Hayes
Pi, Brunswick, Missouri

ONION-MUSHROOM CASSEROLE

3 to 5 onions, thinly sliced, salted
1/2 lb. mushrooms, sliced
2 or 3 stalks celery, chopped
Butter
1/2 lb. Swiss cheese, shredded
1 sm. loaf French bread, sliced
1 can mushroom soup
1/2 c. milk
2 tsp. soy sauce

Saute . . . . . . first 3 ingredients in a small amount of butter in skillet, stirring frequently.
Layer . . . . . . vegetables and cheese in buttered 9 x 13-inch baking dish.
Spread . . . . . bread slices with butter, placing on baking sheet.
Bake . . . . at 350 degrees for 8 minutes.
Arrange . . . . . over cheese.
Mix . . . . soup, milk and soy sauce together in bowl.
Pour . . . . over bread.
Bake . . . . at 350 degrees for 30 minutes.
Yields . . . . . . 6-8 servings.

Deanna Rowe
Xi Epsilon Sigma, Lawrenceburg, Indiana

ONIONS EN CASSEROLE

4 lg. onions, sliced
3 tbsp. butter
3/4 c. shredded Cheddar cheese
2/3 c. buttered bread crumbs

1/2 c. milk
Salt, pepper and paprika to taste

Saute . . . . . . onions in butter in skillet until tender.
Layer . . . . . . onions, cheese and bread crumbs alternately in greased 8-inch square baking dish.
Pour . . . . milk over top.
Sprinkle . . . . with seasonings.
Bake . . . . at 350 degrees for 30 to 45 minutes or until heated through.
Yields . . . . . . 6 servings.

Betty Lou Wright
Preceptor Zeta, Buhl, Idaho

CREOLE BLACK-EYED PEAS

1 1/3 c. sliced onion
1/4 c. margarine, melted
2 cans black-eyed peas, drained
1 20-oz. can tomatoes
1 1/2 c. bread crumbs
1 tsp. salt
1/2 tsp. pepper

Saute . . . . . . onion in margarine in large skillet.
Stir . . . . in remaining ingredients.
Spoon . . . . . . into 2-quart casserole.
Bake . . . . at 350 degrees for 20 to 25 minutes or until bubbly.
Yields . . . . . . 8 servings.

Marguerite Truelove
Preceptor Alpha Delta, Columbia, Tennessee

POTATOES FOR-A-CROWD

20 lb. potatoes, peeled, shredded
4 cans cream of chicken soup
2 soup cans milk
Grated Cheddar cheese to taste
1 onion, shredded
Salt and pepper to taste
1 16-oz. carton sour cream

Combine . . . . all ingredients in large baking pan, mixing well.
Bake . . . . at 350 degrees for 1 1/2 hours.
Yields . . . . . . 20 servings.

Nicki Brennemann
Epsilon Kappa, Hyannis, Nebraska

COMPANY POTATO CASSEROLE

6 med. potatoes, peeled
Salt
1 c. sour cream
1 c. cream of chicken soup
1/4 tsp. each pepper, curry powder
4 hard-boiled eggs, sliced
1/2 c. soft bread crumbs
1/2 c. shredded sharp Cheddar cheese

Cook . . . . potatoes in boiling salted water in saucepan until tender.
Cut . . . . into 1/4-inch slices.
Mix . . . . sour cream, soup, 1 teaspoon salt, pepper and curry powder in bowl.
Layer . . . . . . 1/3 of the potatoes, egg slices and soup mixture in 2-quart casserole.
Repeat . . . . . layers until all ingredients are used.
Toss . . . . bread crumbs and cheese together in bowl.
Sprinkle . . . . over casserole.
Bake . . . . at 350 degrees for 30 minutes.

Madeline Davis
Alpha Phi, Paris, Missouri

BAKED SPINACH

2 eggs, slightly beaten
2 c. milk
1 tsp. salt
2 pkg. frozen chopped spinach, cooked, drained
2/3 c. bread crumbs
1/2 lb. sliced bacon, chopped, crisp-cooked
1 1/2 c. grated Cheddar cheese

Combine . . . . eggs, milk and salt in bowl, mixing well.
Stir . . . . in spinach, bread crumbs, bacon and half the cheese.
Pour . . . . into 1-quart casserole.
Sprinkle . . . . remaining cheese around edge of casserole.
Garnish . . . . . with paprika.
Bake . . . . at 375 degrees for 35 to 45 minutes or until knife inserted in center comes out clean.

Helen A. Heath
Preceptor Upsilon, Muncie, Indiana

CHEESE AND SPINACH CASSEROLE

1 1-lb. carton cottage cheese
3 eggs
1/2 lb. American cheese, cubed
1 tbsp. butter, melted
2 pkg. frozen chopped spinach, thawed
3 tbsp. flour
Pinch of salt

Combine . . . . first 4 ingredients in bowl, mixing well.
Add . . . . spinach, flour and salt, mixing well.
Pour . . . . into buttered 10 x 13-inch baking dish.
Bake . . . . at 350 degrees for 1 hour.
Yields . . . . . . 8 servings.

Ruth Biles
Lambda Xi, Douglasville, Pennsylvania

COMPANY SQUASH CASSEROLE

3 med. yellow squash, chopped
1 med. onion, chopped
5 tbsp. butter, melted
2 tbsp. flour
1 c. milk
5 slices American cheese, chopped
1 3-oz. can mushrooms, drained, chopped
1/2 c. cracker crumbs
1/2 c. chopped pecans

Cook . . . . squash and onion in salted water to cover in saucepan for 5 minutes; drain.
Blend . . . . . . 3 tablespoons butter and flour in small saucepan.
Cook . . . . over low heat for 1 minute, stirring constantly.
Stir . . . . in milk gradually.
Cook . . . . over medium heat until thick, stirring constantly.
Add . . . . cheese.
Cook . . . . over low heat until cheese is melted, stirring constantly.
Combine . . . . with vegetables in large bowl, mixing well.
Spoon . . . . . . into lightly greased 1 1/2-quart casserole.
Toss . . . . cracker crumbs and pecans with remaining butter.

Sprinkle . . . . over casserole.
Bake . . . . at 350 degrees for 30 minutes.
Yields . . . . . . 6 servings.

Betty Pecoraro
Xi Alpha Delta, Pascagoula, Mississippi

SOUTHERN SWEET POTATOES

2 16-oz. cans sweet potatoes
1 c. sugar
2 eggs, beaten
Butter, melted
1 c. packed light brown sugar
1 c. pecans
1/3 c. flour
1/3 c. milk

Mix . . . . first 3 ingredients with 1/4 cup
butter in bowl.
Pour . . . . into 9 x 13-inch baking dish.
Combine . . . . brown sugar, pecans, flour, milk
and 1/3 cup butter in medium
bowl, mixing well.
Pour . . . . over sweet potato mixture.
Bake . . . . at 350 degrees for 30 to 35 minutes or until heated through.

Marjorie A. Ficke
Xi Beta, Lincoln, Nebraska

TOMATO WEDGES PROVENCAL

1/4 c. fine bread crumbs
1/4 c. finely chopped onion
1/4 c. chopped parsley
1 clove of garlic, minced
2 to 3 tbsp. margarine, softened
1/2 tsp. salt
1/8 tsp. pepper
1/4 tsp. basil
4 tomatoes

Combine . . . . all ingredients, except tomatoes,
in bowl, mixing well.
Cut . . . . each tomato into 8 wedges and
arrange in shallow greased bak-
ing dish.
Sprinkle . . . . with crumb mixture.
Bake . . . . at 425 degrees for 5 to 8 minutes or until tomatoes are
tender.

Joan G. McDonald
Laureate Gamma
Vancouver, British Columbia, Canada

ZUCCHINI STUFFING CASSEROLE

4 med. zucchini, cut into 1/2-in. slices
3/4 c. shredded carrot
1/2 c. chopped onion
6 tbsp. butter, melted
2 1/4 c. herb-seasoned stuffing mix
1 can cream of chicken soup
1/2 c. sour cream

Cook . . . . zucchini in salted water in sauce-
pan just until tender; drain.
Saute . . . . . . carrot and onion in 4 table-
spoons butter in saucepan until
tender; remove from heat.
Stir . . . . in 1 1/2 cups stuffing mix, soup,
sour cream and zucchini.
Spoon . . . . . . into 2-quart casserole.
Toss . . . . remaining stuffing mix with 2
tablespoons butter in bowl.
Sprinkle . . . . over casserole.
Bake . . . . at 350 degrees for 30 to 40 min-
utes or until brown.
Yields . . . . . . 6-8 servings.

Dianne Bartholomew
Preceptor Epsilon, Kahului, Maui, Hawaii

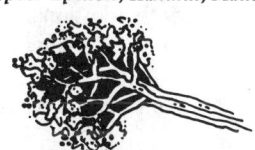

VEGETABLE CASSEROLE DELUXE

1 can mushroom soup
2 hard-boiled eggs, chopped
4 tbsp. milk
Salt and pepper to taste
1 can asparagus
1 can French-style green beans
Italian bread crumbs
Slivered almonds

Combine . . . . first 5 ingredients in bowl, mix-
ing well.
Layer . . . . . . half the asparagus, green beans
and soup mixture in 1 1/2-quart
casserole.
Repeat . . . . . layers.
Top . . . . with bread crumbs and almonds.
Bake . . . . at 350 degrees for 30 minutes.
Yields . . . . . . 6-8 servings.

Mae Gannon
Alpha Alpha, Spokane, Washington

VEGETABLE-NOODLE CASSEROLE

3 onions, sliced
1 clove of garlic, chopped
1 c. minced parsley
1/4 tsp. oregano
4 tbsp. butter, melted
2 tbsp. olive oil
4 tomatoes, peeled, seeded, chopped
1 c. chicken broth
Salt and pepper to taste
1 lb. wide noodles, cooked
3 sm. zucchini, sliced
Grated Cheddar cheese

Saute ...... onions and garlic with parsley and oregano in 2 tablespoons butter and olive oil in heavy saucepan until onions are golden.
Add .... tomatoes, chicken broth and salt and pepper to taste.
Cook .... for 10 minutes.
Combine .... noodles and remaining butter.
Stir .... in tomato sauce and zucchini.
Pour .... into buttered baking dish.
Sprinkle .... with cheese.
Dot .... with additional butter.
Bake .... at 375 degrees for 15 to 20 minutes.

Photograph for this recipe on page 89.

VEGETABLE MEDLEY

2 c. cut green beans
2 c. sliced celery
2 c. coarsely shredded cabbage
1/4 c. flour
1/4 c. melted butter
2 c. milk
Cheddar cheese, shredded
Salt and pepper to taste
2 tomatoes, peeled, thickly sliced

Cook .... beans in water in saucepan until tender-crisp.
Add .... celery and cabbage.
Cook .... for 2 to 3 minutes longer or until celery is tender-crisp; drain well.
Blend ...... flour and butter in saucepan.
Stir .... in milk.
Cook .... until smooth and thick, stirring constantly.

Add .... 1 cup cheese.
Cook .... over low heat until cheese melts, stirring constantly.
Season .... with salt and pepper.
Fold .... in cooked vegetables.
Place .... in buttered shallow baking dish.
Top .... with tomato slices.
Sprinkle .... with salt, pepper and additional cheese.
Bake .... at 400 degrees for 12 to 15 minutes or until lightly browned.

Photograph for this recipe above.

SAVORY SUCCOTASH

1 16-oz. can French-style green beans, drained
1 16-oz. can whole kernel corn, drained
1/2 c. mayonnaise
1/2 c. shredded sharp Cheddar cheese
1/2 c. each chopped celery, green pepper
2 tbsp. chopped onion
1 c. bread crumbs
2 tbsp. melted butter

Combine .... first 7 ingredients in bowl, mixing well.
Spoon ...... into 2-quart baking dish.
Toss .... bread crumbs with butter in bowl.
Sprinkle .... over top.
Bake .... at 350 degrees for 30 minutes.
Yields ...... 8-10 servings.

Frances Anewalt
Life Member at Large, Dayton, Ohio

Side Dishes

OVEN OMELET BRUNCH

18 eggs, beaten
1 c. sour cream
1 c. milk
2 tsp. salt
1/4 c. chopped green onions
1/4 c. butter, melted

Combine .... first 4 ingredients in large bowl, beating well.
Stir .... in onions.
Pour .... over butter in 9 x 13-inch baking dish.
Bake .... at 325 degrees for 35 minutes or until eggs are set but moist.
Serve .... immediately with Canadian bacon and sweet rolls.
Yields ...... 12 servings.

Mary Kathryn Fithian
Xi Gamma Alpha, Sacramento, California

DELICIOUS BARLEY CASSEROLE

1 c. quick-cooking fine barley
1 med. onion, chopped
Melted butter
1/2 c. slivered almonds
1 2-oz. package dry onion soup mix
2 c. chicken broth
3/4 to 1 c. sliced mushrooms
1 5-oz. can water chestnuts, drained, sliced

Saute ...... barley and onion in butter in saucepan until light golden.
Add .... almonds, soup mix and broth, mixing well.
Saute ...... mushrooms in a small amount of butter in small skillet.
Stir .... into barley mixture.
Add .... water chestnuts, mixing well.
Spoon ...... into 2-quart casserole.
Bake .... covered, at 350 degrees for 1 hour.
Yields ...... 6 servings.

Denise Adams
Delta Zeta, Drumright, Oklahoma

MACARONI-CHICKEN CASSEROLE

1/2 c. chopped celery
1 16-oz. package elbow macaroni
1 can cream of mushroom soup
2 c. chopped chicken
1 can cream of celery soup
3 hard-boiled eggs, chopped
1 med. onion, finely chopped
2 c. cubed Velveeta cheese
1/2 c. frozen peas
1 pt. half and half

Cook .... celery in a small amount of water in saucepan until tender-crisp; drain.
Layer ...... next 6 ingredients, celery, cheese and peas in order given in greased 9 x 13-inch casserole.
Pour .... half and half over all.
Chill .... covered, overnight.
Bake .... at 350 degrees for 1 hour.
Yields ...... 10-12 servings.

Cleanne Schieber
Beta Iota, Iowa City, Iowa

CUERNAVACA CASSEROLE

1 c. yellow cornmeal
3/4 tsp. salt
1/2 tsp. baking powder
1 c. milk
2 eggs, slightly beaten
1/4 c. oil
2 c. cooked rice
2 c. shredded Cheddar cheese
1 17-oz. can cream-style corn
1 3 1/4-oz. can sliced olives
1 med. onion, chopped
1 can chopped green chilies
4 drops of Tabasco sauce

Combine .... cornmeal, salt and baking powder in large bowl, mixing well.
Add .... remaining ingredients, stirring just until blended.
Pour .... into well-greased 12-inch casserole.
Bake .... at 350 degrees for 40 to 50 minutes or until set.
Yields ...... 8-10 servings.

Yvonne Clapp
Preceptor Zeta Phi, Sunnyvale, California

MANICOTTI-CHILI CASSEROLE

1/4 c. chopped onion
1 clove of garlic, minced
1 tbsp. oil
2 cans chili-beef soup
2 eggs, beaten
2 1/2 c. cottage cheese
1 or 2 jalapeno peppers, chopped
1 1/2 c. shredded sharp Cheddar cheese
12 manicotti shells, cooked, drained

Saute ...... onion with garlic in oil in skillet until tender.
Stir .... in soup and 1/2 cup water.
Cook .... until heated through.
Combine .... eggs, cottage cheese, peppers and 1 cup Cheddar cheese in bowl, mixing well.
Spoon ...... cheese mixture into manicotti shells.
Pour .... half the soup mixture into 7 1/2 x 12-inch baking dish.
Arrange ..... shells in prepared baking dish.
Pour .... remaining soup mixture over top.
Bake .... covered, at 350 degrees for 40 to 45 minutes or until bubbly.
Sprinkle .... remaining 1/2 cup Cheddar cheese over top.
Bake .... uncovered, for 2 to 3 minutes or until cheese is melted.
Let .... stand for 5 minutes.
Garnish ..... with sliced ripe olives and green onion.

Jan Semsak
Preceptor Alpha Chi, Puyallup Washington
Margaret Katter
Xi Alpha Upsilon, Garner, Iowa

THAI RICE

8 to 10 slices bacon
1 med. head cabbage, chopped
1 white onion, chopped
1 green pepper, chopped
6 to 8 green onions with tops, chopped
3 cloves of garlic, chopped
Soy sauce and hot sauce to taste
Salt and pepper to taste
1 c. rice, cooked
3 pieces of chicken, cooked, chopped

Cook .... bacon in skillet until crisp; remove and set aside.
Stir .... 1 cup water and remaining ingredients except rice and chicken into pan drippings.
Simmer ..... covered, until cabbage is tender.
Stir .... in rice, chicken and crumbled bacon.
Cook .... until heated through.
Yields ...... 6 servings.

Mary Frances Brown
Preceptor Mu, Cushing Oklahoma

WILD RICE AND TOMATOES

1 pkg. wild rice
1/2 lb. mushrooms
1/2 c. onion
1/4 c. each chopped red and green pepper
1 19-oz. can tomatoes
1/2 lb. grated mozzarella cheese
1 tsp. salt

Soak .... wild rice in water in bowl overnight; drain.
Prepare ..... rice using package directions.
Saute ...... mushrooms, onion and peppers in a small amount of oil in skillet.
Add .... tomatoes, cheese, salt and rice, mixing well.
Spoon ...... into buttered 3-quart casserole.
Bake .... at 350 degrees for 1 hour.
Yields ...... 4-6 servings.

Susan Champagne
Xi Epsilon Alpha, Tecumseh, Ontario, Canada

CURRIED RICE

3 c. cooked rice
1/2 stick margarine, melted
1 tsp. curry powder
1 1/2 tsp. salt
1 4-oz. can mushrooms, drained
1/4 c. chopped ripe olives
1/2 c. raisins
1/2 c. slivered almonds

Combine .... all ingredients in bowl, mixing well.
Spoon ...... into 2-quart casserole.
Bake .... at 350 degrees until heated through.

Barbara G. Hood
Beta Sigma Phi XP 994, Hampton, South Carolina

Breads & Desserts

Breads

CASEROLE BREAD

4 tbsp. sesame seed
1 egg, beaten
1 1/2 c. milk
3 3/4 c. biscuit mix
1 c. shredded mild Cheddar cheese
1 tbsp. dried chives

Sprinkle .... sesame seed over sides and bottom of greased 2-quart casserole.
Beat .... remaining ingredients in mixer bowl on medium speed for 30 seconds.
Pour .... into prepared casserole.
Bake .... at 350 degrees for 45 minutes or until bread tests done.
Invert ...... onto serving plate.
Yields ...... 6 servings.

Jeanette Azar
Preceptor Beta Zeta, Mt. Clemens, Michigan

CREOLE CASSEROLE BREAD

1 c. milk, scalded
3 tbsp. dark brown sugar
1 tbsp. salt
2 tbsp. margarine
2 pkg. yeast
1 tsp. cinnamon
1/2 tsp. nutmeg
4 c. flour

Combine .... milk, brown sugar, salt and margarine in saucepan; cool to lukewarm.
Dissolve .... yeast in 1 cup warm water in bowl.
Add .... milk mixture, cinnamon, nutmeg and flour.
Stir .... for 2 minutes.
Let .... rise, covered, for 1 hour or until doubled in bulk.
Stir .... batter down, beating for 1/2 minute.
Pour .... into greased 1 1/2-quart casserole.
Bake .... at 375 degrees for 1 hour or until bread tests done.

Photograph for this recipe on page 101.

EASY BEER BREAD

3 c. self-rising flour
3 tbsp. sugar
8 oz. beer, at room temperature

Combine .... all ingredients in bowl, beating well.
Pour .... into greased loaf pan.
Bake .... at 400 degrees for 40 to 50 minutes or until bread tests done.
Yields ...... 6 servings.

Patricia S. Beittel
Preceptor Alpha Gamma, Carlisle, Pennsylvania

STEAM BREAD

2 c. self-rising cornmeal
1 c. self-rising flour
1/2 c. sugar
2 eggs
2 c. buttermilk
1/2 c. oil

Combine .... all ingredients in order given in large bowl, mixing well after each addition.
Pour .... into large baking dish.
Cover ...... allowing room for rising.
Bake .... at 350 degrees for 45 minutes.

Willa Reynolds
Xi Upsilon, Paris, Tennessee

BREAKFAST BUBBLE

1/2 c. chopped nuts
1 pkg. frozen rolls
1/2 stick butter, melted
1/2 c. packed brown sugar

Sprinkle .... nuts over bottom of bundt pan.
Dip .... each roll in butter.
Coat .... with brown sugar.
Place .... in bundt pan.
Let .... rise, covered, in warm place overnight.
Bake .... covered, at 350 degrees for 30 to 40 minutes or until golden brown.
Turn .... out on serving plate.

Cheryl Kay Buchholtz
Rho, Peoria, Arizona

MONKEY BREAD

Nuts (opt.)
2 c. packed brown sugar
2 tsp. cinnamon
4 pkg. refrigerator buttermilk
*   biscuits, quartered*
1 1/2 sticks butter, melted

Place . . . . nuts in bottom of greased bundt
pan.
Mix . . . . 1 cup brown sugar and cinna-
mon in bowl.
Roll . . . . . . biscuit quarters in brown sugar
mixture.
Layer . . . . . . in bundt pan.
Blend . . . . . remaining 1 cup brown sugar
with butter.
Pour . . . . over biscuits.
Bake . . . . . . at 400 degrees for 5 minutes.
Reduce . . . . . temperature to 350 degrees.
Bake . . . . . . for 20 to 25 minutes or until
bread tests done.
Invert . . . . . . onto serving plate.
Yields . . . . . . 12-14 servings.

Naomi Morrow
Preceptor Laureate, Pottsville, Pennsylvania

SOUR CREAM COFFEE CAKE

1 c. margarine
2 c. sugar
2 eggs
1 c. sour cream
1/2 tsp. vanilla extract
2 c. flour
1 tsp. baking powder
1/2 tsp. salt
Nuts
2 tbsp. brown sugar
1 tsp. cinnamon

Cream . . . . . . margarine, sugar and eggs in
large bowl.
Fold . . . . in sour cream and vanilla.
Add . . . . dry ingredients and 1/2 cup nuts
if desired, mixing well.
Mix . . . . brown sugar, cinnamon and 3/4
cup nuts in small bowl.
Layer . . . . . . batter and nut mixture alternately in greased and floured
bundt pan ending with nut
mixture.

Bake . . . . at 350 degrees for 1 hour.
Turn . . . . onto serving plate.
Yields . . . . . . 10-12 servings.

Janet Engle
Xi Gamma Theta, Norfolk, Nebraska

APPLESAUCE BREAD

1/2 c. shortening, softened
1 lg. egg
2 1/2 c. flour
3/4 tsp. cinnamon
1/2 tsp. each allspice, cloves
1/2 c. chopped citron
1 1/2 c. sugar
1 c. applesauce
1 1/2 tsp. soda
1 c. raisins

Combine . . . . all ingredients with 1 to 1 1/2
cups water in large bowl, mixing
well.
Pour . . . . into well-greased loaf pan.
Let . . . . stand for 20 minutes.
Bake . . . . at 350 degrees for 60 to 70 minutes or until bread tests done.

Gracia L. Lee
Preceptor Beta Upsilon, Hutchinson, Kansas

MINCEMEAT-BANANA BREAD

3/4 c. oil
2 c. mashed bananas
1/2 c. chopped apple
2 1/2 c. flour
4 tsp. soda
1 1/2 c. packed brown sugar
1 tsp. salt
4 eggs, well beaten
1 c. mincemeat
1/3 c. chopped nuts

Mix . . . . all ingredients together in large
bowl.
Pour . . . . into prepared 9 x 13-inch baking
pan.
Bake . . . . at 350 degrees for 1 hour or
until bread tests done.

Jacqueline J. Madden
Xi Phi, Montgomery, Alabama

BANANA-WALNUT BREAD

1/2 c. margarine, softened
1 c. sugar
2 eggs
1 c. mashed ripe bananas
1/4 tsp. soda
2 c. sifted flour
1 tsp. baking powder
1 c. coarsely chopped walnuts

Cream . . . . . . margarine and sugar together in bowl.
Add . . . . eggs 1 at a time, beating well after each addition.
Mix . . . . in bananas.
Add . . . . soda dissolved in 1 tablespoon water, mixing well.
Sift . . . . flour and baking powder into banana mixture, stirring until just mixed.
Stir . . . . in walnuts.
Pour . . . . into greased 5 x 9-inch loaf pan.
Let . . . . stand for 20 minutes.
Bake . . . . at 350 degrees for 1 hour or until bread tests done.

Leona Moore
Xi Alpha Theta, Frankfort, Kentucky

ZUCCHINI-BANANA NUT BREAD

8 c. sugar
1/2 c. shortening
1/2 c. margarine, softened
8 tsp. egg substitute
1   13 1/4-oz. can crushed pineapple
8 c. grated seeded zucchini
2 c. mashed bananas
24 c. sifted flour
1/2 c. baking powder
4 tsp. baking soda
8 tsp. salt
1 tsp. cinnamon
2 c. chopped nuts (opt.)

Combine . . . . first 4 ingredients and 1 cup water in very large bowl, mixing well.

Stir . . . . in pineapple, zucchini and bananas.
Sift . . . . dry ingredients together.
Add . . . . . . to zucchini mixture with nuts, mixing well.
Pour . . . . . . into 8 greased loaf pans.
Let . . . . stand at room temperature for 20 minutes before baking.
Bake . . . . . . at 350 degrees for 1 hour and 10 minutes.
Yields . . . . . . 8 loaves.

Jane Neal
Preceptor Kappa, Powell, Wyoming

BLUEBERRY BREAKFAST BREAD

1 pkg. blueberry muffin mix
1/2 c. sugar
1/4 c. flour
2 tbsp. butter, softened

Prepare . . . . . muffin mix using package directions.
Pour . . . . into greased 9-inch round baking dish.
Combine . . . . sugar and flour in bowl, mixing well.
Cut . . . . in butter until crumbly.
Sprinkle . . . . over batter.
Bake . . . . at 400 degrees for 30 minutes or until bread tests done.
Serve . . . . . . warm with butter.
Yields . . . . . . 6 servings.

Pat Pence
Xi Alpha Theta, Frankfort, Kentucky

BUTTER BRICKLE BREAD

1 box butter brickle cake mix
1 pkg. coconut instant pudding mix
1/4 c. poppy seed
1/4 c. oil
4 eggs

Combine . . . . all ingredients and 1 cup warm water in bowl, mixing well.
Pour . . . . into 2 greased and floured 4 x 8-inch loaf pans.
Bake . . . . at 350 degrees for 30 minutes.
Yields . . . . . . 2 loaves.

Virginia L. Hunter
Preceptor Gamma Phi, Springfield, Missouri

DEEP DARK CHOCOLATE TEA BREAD

2 c. sifted flour
1 tbsp. baking powder
1/3 c. cocoa
1/2 tsp. salt
3/4 c. sugar
1 egg, slightly beaten
1 c. milk
3 tbsp. shortening, melted
1/3 c. semi-sweet chocolate chips

Sift . . . . first 5 ingredients together into bowl.
Beat . . . . . . egg, milk and shortening together in bowl.
Add . . . . . . to flour mixture, stirring until just moistened.
Fold . . . . . . in chocolate chips.
Pour . . . . . . into greased 5 x 9-inch loaf pan.
Bake . . . . . . at 350 degrees for 1 hour.
Yields . . . . . . 12-16 servings.

Jeannette Richardson
Preceptor Gamma Mu, Lubbock, Texas

CINNAMON POTATO-NUT BREAD

3/4 c. sugar
2 tbsp. shortening
1 egg
3/4 c. riced cooked potatoes
1 1/4 c. potato water
2/3 c. nonfat dry milk
3 c. flour
1 tbsp. baking powder
1/2 tsp. salt
2 tsp. cinnamon
1 c. nuts
3/4 c. raisins

Mix . . . . first 4 ingredients in large bowl.
Stir . . . . in potato water.
Combine . . . . next 5 dry ingredients.
Add . . . . . . to potato mixture, mixing well.
Fold . . . . . . in nuts and raisins.
Pour . . . . . . into greased loaf pan.
Bake . . . . . . at 350 degrees for 60 to 70 minutes or until bread tests done.

Maria Rost
Xi Beta Alpha, American Falls, Idaho

HOBO BREAD

1 1/2 c. raisins
1 egg
2 tbsp. molasses
1 c. packed brown sugar
1 tbsp. oil
2 1/2 c. sifted flour
1/2 tsp. salt
2 tsp. soda

Combine . . . . raisins with 1 1/2 cups water in saucepan.
Boil . . . . for 1 minute; cool.
Combine . . . . with remaining ingredients in bowl, mixing well.
Spoon . . . . . . into 2 greased and floured loaf pans.
Bake . . . . . . at 325 degrees for 1 hour.
Yields . . . . . . 2 loaves.

Penny Stahl
Xi Alpha Rho, Custer, South Dakota

PEACH BREAD

1 1/2 c. sugar
1/2 c. shortening
2 eggs
2 1/4 c. fresh peach puree
2 c. flour
1 tsp. each cinnamon, soda, baking powder
1/4 tsp. salt
1 tsp. vanilla extract
1 c. finely chopped pecans

Cream . . . . . . sugar and shortening together in bowl.
Add . . . . eggs, mixing well.
Stir . . . . in peach puree.
Add . . . . . . next 5 dry ingredients, mixing well.
Blend . . . . . . in vanilla and pecans.
Pour . . . . . . into 2 greased and floured loaf pans.
Bake . . . . . . at 325 degrees for 55 to 60 minutes or until bread tests done.
Let . . . . stand for several minutes before removing from pans.
Yields . . . . . . 2 loaves.

Dorothy Clarkson
Xi Iota Beta X5619, Union, Missouri

POPPY SEED BREAD

1 pkg. coconut instant pudding mix
1 pkg. yellow cake mix
1/4 c. poppy seed
1/2 c. oil
4 eggs

Combine .... first 4 ingredients with 1 cup boiling water in bowl, mixing well.
Beat .... for 2 minutes.
Add .... eggs 1 at a time, beating well after each addition.
Pour .... into prepared loaf pans.
Bake .... at 350 degrees for 35 to 50 minutes or until bread tests done.
Yields ...... 2 loaves.

Beth M. Caillet
Eta Upsilon, Lawton, Oklahoma

PUMPKIN BREAD

2 eggs
1/2 c. oil
1 c. canned pumpkin
1 1/4 c. sugar
1 1/2 c. flour
1/4 tsp. salt
1/2 tsp. each nutmeg, cinnamon
1 tsp. soda
1/2 c. chopped walnuts
1/2 c. chopped candied cherries

Combine .... eggs, oil and pumpkin with 1/3 cup water in large bowl.
Sift .... dry ingredients together.
Beat .... into pumpkin mixture.
Stir .... in walnuts and cherries.
Pour .... into greased and floured loaf pan.
Bake .... at 350 degrees for 1 hour.

Brenda C. Taylor
Xi Alpha Xi, Memphis, Tennessee

STRAWBERRY BREAD

3 c. flour
1 tsp. each soda, salt, cinnamon
2 c. sugar
4 eggs, beaten
1 1/4 c. oil
1 16-oz. package frozen strawberries, thawed
1 1/4 c. chopped pecans

Sift .... first 5 ingredients together.
Mix .... eggs, oil and strawberries in large bowl.
Add .... sifted ingredients, mixing well.
Fold .... in pecans.
Pour .... into 2 prepared loaf pans.
Bake .... at 350 degrees for 1 hour or until bread tests done.
Yields ...... 10-12 servings.

Carol Petersen
Xi Zeta, APO, New York

ZUCCHINI BREAD

4 c. coarsely shredded zucchini
3 c. flour
2 c. sugar
1 1/4 c. oil
4 eggs, beaten
4 tsp. vanilla extract
1 tbsp. cinnamon
1 1/2 tsp. each salt, soda
1/2 tsp. baking powder
1 c. chopped nuts

Combine .... all ingredients in mixer bowl.
Beat .... on low speed for 1 minute.
Grease ...... bottom of two 5 x 9-inch loaf pans.
Pour .... batter into prepared pans.
Bake .... at 325 degrees for 50 to 60 minutes or until bread tests done.
Cool .... for 10 minutes before removing from pans.
Yields ...... 2 loaves.

Mary Ann Watson
Iota Tau, Macomb, Illinois

Desserts

SCALLOPED APPLESAUCE

4 slices bread, toasted, cubed
1/3 c. melted butter
1 16-oz. jar chunky applesauce
1/3 c. sugar
1 tsp. lemon juice
1/2 tsp. grated lemon rind

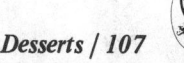

Combine .... bread and butter in bowl, tossing to mix.
Stir .... in remaining ingredients.
Spoon ...... into 1-quart casserole.
Bake .... at 350 degrees for 1/2 hour.
Yields ...... 4-6 servings.

Photograph for this recipe above.

APPLE CRISP

1/3 c. sifted flour
1 c. quick oats
1/2 c. packed brown sugar
1/2 tsp. salt
1 tsp. cinnamon
1/3 c. melted butter
4 c. sliced apples
1 tsp. lemon juice

Combine .... first 5 ingredients in bowl.
Add .... butter, mixing well.
Place .... apples in shallow greased baking dish.
Sprinkle .... with lemon juice.
Top .... with oats mixture.
Bake .... at 375 degrees for 30 minutes.
Yields ...... 4-6 servings.

Margaret Abel
Xi Beta Kappa, Nashville, Tennessee

APRICOT CASSEROLE

2 13-oz. cans apricot halves, drained
2/3 c. packed brown sugar
2 tubes Ritz crackers, crushed
1/2 c. melted butter

Layer ...... first 3 ingredients in order given in greased 8-inch square baking pan.
Drizzle ..... butter evenly over top.
Bake .... at 325 degrees for 30 minutes.
Yields ...... 6-8 servings.

Martha Bein
Xi Zeta Lambda, Aurora, Illinois

BAKED FRUIT

2 cans pineapple chunks, drained
1 lg. can each pears, peaches, apricots, drained
1 sm. jar maraschino cherries, drained
1/2 c. packed brown sugar
1/2 tsp. each cloves, allspice
1/4 tsp. cinnamon
1/2 stick butter, melted

Combine .... fruits in 9 x 13-inch baking dish.
Mix .... brown sugar and spices with butter.
Pour .... over fruit, mixing lightly.
Bake .... at 350 degrees for 30 minutes.

Carolyn Ann Lowe
Preceptor Gamma, Baytown, Texas

BANANA-GRAPE CASSEROLE

4 bananas, thickly sliced
Juice and grated rind of 1/2 lemon
1/4 c. sugar
Pinch of salt
1 tsp. cinnamon
1/4 tsp. nutmeg
1/2 c. seedless grapes
2 tbsp. butter

Combine .... bananas with lemon juice and rind in bowl, mixing lightly.
Mix .... sugar with next 3 ingredients in small bowl.
Layer ...... banana mixture, sugar mixture and grapes alternately in greased 8 x 8-inch casserole until all ingredients are used.
Dot .... with butter.
Bake .... at 375 degrees for 20 minutes.
Yields ...... 4 servings.

Martha Browning
Preceptor Alpha, Little Rock, Arkansas

ALL-TOGETHER BLUEBERRY DIET BREAKFAST

8 slices diet white bread, toasted, cubed
2 c. blueberries
2 c. low-fat milk
4 eggs, beaten
3 pkg. artificial sweetener
1 1/2 tsp. vanilla extract
1 tsp. cinnamon

Layer ...... half the bread cubes and all the blueberries in 8 x 8-inch baking dish.
Top .... with remaining bread cubes.
Combine .... remaining 5 ingredients in blender container.
Process ..... until blended.
Pour .... over casserole.
Bake .... at 350 degrees for 35 minutes.
Yields ...... 4 servings.

Betty L. Leib
Preceptor Sigma, Harrisburg, Pennsylvania

GEORGE'S CHERRY CRISP

2 tbsp. butter
1/4 c. flour
1/4 c. quick oats
1/4 c. packed light brown sugar
1/2 tsp. cinnamon
1/8 tsp. nutmeg
1 can cherry pie filling

Cut .... butter into flour in bowl until crumbly.
Add .... next 4 ingredients, mixing well.
Layer ...... pie filling and oat mixture in 8-inch square baking pan.
Bake .... at 350 degrees for 30 minutes or until bubbly.
Serve .... with whipped topping.
Yields ...... 6 servings.

Joan Graham
Preceptor Alpha Delta, Columbia, Tennessee

PEACH DELIGHT

1 30-oz. can peach slices
2 tbsp. cornstarch
1/4 tsp. salt
1/2 c. sugar
1 tbsp. lemon juice
Almond extract

2 eggs, separated
1/4 tsp. each cream of tartar, cinnamon
1/4 c. flour
1/4 c. chopped pecans

Drain ...... peaches, reserving syrup.
Mix .... cornstarch, salt and 1/4 cup sugar in saucepan.
Stir .... in reserved syrup.
Cook .... until thick, stirring constantly; remove from heat.
Stir .... in lemon juice and several drops of almond extract.
Add .... peaches, reserving a few slices for garnish.
Beat .... egg whites with cream of tartar and cinnamon in bowl for 1 minute or until soft peaks form.
Add .... remaining 1/4 cup sugar gradually, beating for 3 minutes or until stiff peaks form.
Beat .... egg yolks for 4 minutes or until thick and lemon colored.
Fold .... egg yolks and flour into egg whites in order given.
Bring .... peach mixture to a boil.
Spoon ...... into 1 1/2-quart casserole.
Spread ..... egg batter evenly to edges.
Sprinkle .... with pecans.
Bake .... at 350 degrees for 40 minutes.
Garnish ..... with reserved peach slices.
Yields ...... 6-8 servings.

Frances Kucera
Laureate Omicron, Eugene, Oregon

PEACHES SUPREME

8 canned peach halves
2 tbsp. melted butter
1/2 c. mincemeat

Arrange ..... peach halves in buttered baking dish.
Brush ...... with melted butter.
Spoon ...... 1 tablespoon mincemeat into each half and remaining mincemeat around peaches.
Bake .... at 350 degrees for 15 to 20 minutes or until lightly browned.
Serve .... with sour cream.
Yields ...... 4-8 servings.

Photograph for this recipe on page 6.

EASY PEACH COBBLER

Sugar
1 c. flour
2 tsp. baking powder
1/8 tsp. salt
2 tsp. vanilla extract
2/3 c. milk
1/4 c. butter
4 c. sliced peaches
1/2 tsp. cinnamon

Mix .... 1 cup sugar and next 4 ingredients in bowl.
Add .... milk, beating until smooth.
Melt .... butter in 2-quart casserole.
Pour .... batter over butter.
Spoon ...... peaches over batter.
Sprinkle .... with 1 tablespoon sugar and cinnamon.
Bake .... at 350 degrees for 1 hour.
Serve .... hot with cream.
Yields ...... 6 servings.

Phyllis A. Cooper
Laureate Alpha, Huntsville, Alabama

AUNT BESSIE'S STRAWBERRY AND RHUBARB PIE

4 c. flour
2 c. packed brown sugar
1 1/3 c. butter, softened
3 c. sugar
4 tbsp. (heaping) cornstarch
1/2 tsp. cinnamon
12 c. chopped rhubarb
4 c. sliced strawberries

Mix .... first 2 ingredients together in bowl.
Cut .... in butter until crumbly.
Press .... into 10 x 15-inch baking dish, reserving 1 cup mixture.
Combine .... sugar, cornstarch, cinnamon and 2 cups cold water in large saucepan, mixing well.
Cook .... until thick, stirring constantly.
Stir .... in rhubarb and strawberries.
Pour .... into prepared baking dish.
Sprinkle .... with reserved flour mixture.
Bake .... at 375 degrees for 30 minutes.
Yields ...... 20 servings.

Beverly Scott
Preceptor Omicron, Elma, Washington

PINEAPPLE-CHEESE CASSEROLE

1 20-oz. can pineapple chunks
1/2 c. sugar
3 tbsp. flour
1 c. shredded Cheddar cheese
1/4 c. melted margarine
1/2 c. Ritz cracker crumbs

Drain ...... pineapple, reserving 3 tablespoons juice.
Combine .... sugar, flour and reserved juice in bowl, mixing well.
Stir .... in cheese and pineapple.
Spoon ...... into greased 1-quart casserole.
Combine .... margarine and cracker crumbs in bowl, mixing well.
Sprinkle .... over pineapple mixture.
Bake .... at 350 degrees for 20 to 30 minutes or until lightly browned.
Yields ...... 4-6 servings.

Sue Stein
Delta Beta, Greensboro, North Carolina

NIGHT-BEFORE FRENCH TOAST

1 10-oz. long loaf French bread, sliced 1-in. thick
8 lg. eggs
3 c. milk
6 tbsp. sugar
3/4 tsp. salt
1 tsp. vanilla extract
6 tbsp. butter
Cinnamon to taste

Arrange ..... bread in well-buttered 9 x 13-inch baking dish.
Combine .... next 5 ingredients in bowl, mixing well.
Pour .... over bread.
Chill .... covered, for 4 to 36 hours.
Dot .... with butter and sprinkle with cinnamon.
Place .... in cold oven.
Bake .... at 350 degrees for 45 to 50 minutes.
Serve .... with syrup, honey, fruit-flavored yogurt or sour cream and fresh fruit.

Meri-Louise Sutton
Xi Omicron, Bluefield, West Virginia

EASY BREAD PUDDING

2 eggs, slightly beaten
2 1/4 c. milk
1 tsp. vanilla extract
1 tbsp. vanilla pudding mix
1 tsp. cinnamon
1/4 tsp. salt
2 c. cubed day-old bread
1/2 c. packed brown sugar
1/2 c. raisins

Combine . . . . first 6 ingredients in bowl, mixing well.
Stir . . . . in bread.
Add . . . . brown sugar and raisins, mixing well.
Spoon . . . . . . into 8-inch round cake pan.
Place . . . . in baking pan of 1-inch hot water.
Bake . . . . at 350 degrees for 45 minutes or until knife inserted between center and edge comes out clean.
Yields . . . . . . 6 servings.

Connie M. Mose
Xi Alpha Pi, Hagerstown, Maryland

GRANDMA'S CHOCOLATE BREAD PUDDING

4 eggs
3 c. milk, scalded
2 c. bread crumbs
1 sq. unsweetened chocolate, melted
Sugar
1 tsp. vanilla extract

Mix . . . . 2 beaten eggs with next 3 ingredients and 2/3 cup sugar.
Pour . . . . into greased 1 1/2-quart casserole.
Bake . . . . at 325 degrees for 45 minutes or until knive inserted in center comes out clean.
Separate . . . . remaining 2 eggs.
Add . . . . 1/2 cup sugar to stiffly beaten egg whites, beating until very stiff.
Beat . . . . in egg yolks and vanilla.
Serve . . . . immediately over warm pudding.
Yields . . . . . . 6-8 servings.

Elizabeth J. Beaverstock
Xi Theta, Hudson, New Hampshire

CARAMEL-TOPPED RICE PUDDING

3 eggs, slightly beaten
1/2 c. sugar
3/4 tsp. salt
1/2 tsp. nutmeg
3 c. milk
1/4 c. butter
1 c. cooked rice
1 tsp. vanilla extract
1/2 tsp. rum extract
1/3 c. slivered almonds
1/2 c. packed brown sugar

Combine . . . . first 4 ingredients in bowl, mixing well.
Scald . . . . milk with 2 tablespoons butter in saucepan.
Add . . . . to egg mixture in fine stream, stirring constantly.
Stir . . . . in rice and flavorings.
Pour . . . . into shallow 1 1/2-quart casserole.
Place . . . . in shallow pan of hot water.
Bake . . . . at 350 degrees for 1/2 hour or until knife inserted near center comes out clean.
Remove . . . . custard from oven and hot water.
Brown . . . . . . almonds in remaining 2 tablespoons butter in skillet.
Stir . . . . in brown sugar.
Sprinkle . . . . over top of custard.
Broil . . . . 3 inches from heat source until topping is hot and bubbly.
Serve . . . . warm or chilled.
Yields . . . . . . 6-8 servings.

Photograph for this recipe above.

DATE PUDDING

1 1/2 c. packed brown sugar
1 1/4 c. flour
1 c. sugar
1 c. chopped dates
1/2 c. chopped pecans
1 tsp. baking powder
1 tsp. vanilla extract
1 c. milk

Dissolve .... brown sugar in 2 cups boiling water in 8 x 12-inch baking pan.
Combine .... flour with next 4 ingredients in large bowl, stirring until dates are well coated.
Stir .... vanilla into milk.
Add .... to date mixture, mixing well.
Pour .... into center of prepared baking pan.
Bake .... at 350 degrees for 45 minutes.
Serve .... with whipped topping.
Yields ...... 16-20 servings.

Lenore Hunt
Preceptor Kappa, Montrose, Colorado

NOODLE PUDDING

1 10-oz. package wide noodles, cooked
3 eggs, beaten
1/4 c. melted butter
1/2 tsp. cinnamon
1/4 tsp. salt
2 lg. apples, peeled, sliced
1/2 c. raisins
1/2 c. orange marmalade

Combine .... all ingredients in bowl, mixing well.
Place .... in greased 9 x 13-inch baking dish.
Bake .... at 350 degrees for 45 to 60 minutes or until brown.
Yields ...... 6-8 servings.

Linda Schwartzberg
Xi Iota Kappa, St. Peters, Missouri

TASTY HASTY PUDDING

1 1/2 c. packed brown sugar
1 c. flour

2 tsp. baking powder
1/2 tsp. salt
1/2 c. milk
1/2 c. currants
1 tsp. vanilla extract
1 tbsp. margarine
1/2 tsp. nutmeg

Combine .... 1/2 cup brown sugar with next 5 ingredients in bowl, mixing well.
Place .... in large greased casserole.
Combine .... vanilla, margarine, nutmeg and remaining 1 cup brown sugar with 2 cups boiling water in saucepan, mixing well.
Bring .... to a boil.
Pour .... over mixture in casserole.
Bake .... at 350 degrees for 30 minutes.
Serve .... warm with cream.
Yields ...... 6 servings.

Vivian D. Myers
Preceptor Delta Beta, Norwalk, California

ORANGE PUDDING CAKE

1 c. sugar
2 tbsp. butter
1 1/2 tbsp. grated orange rind
4 eggs, separated
1/4 c. flour
1 1/4 c. milk
1/2 c. orange juice

Cream ...... 1/2 cup sugar, butter and orange rind together in large bowl.
Add .... egg yolks 1 at a time, beating well after each addition.
Blend ...... in flour, milk and orange juice gradually.
Beat .... egg whites in bowl until soft peaks form.
Add .... remaining 1/2 cup sugar, beating until stiff.
Fold .... into orange mixture.
Spoon ...... into buttered 1 1/2-quart casserole.
Bake .... at 350 degrees for 1 hour or until set.
Serve .... warm or cold.
Yields ...... 6 servings.

Mary E. Oakley
Laureate Mu, Orlando, Florida

APPLE DUMP CAKE

1 can apples
1 box spice cake mix
3/4 c. packed brown sugar
1 c. chopped pecans
2 sticks margarine, sliced

Layer . . . . . . all ingredients in order given in 9 x 13-inch baking pan.
Bake . . . . at 325 degrees for 1 hour.
Serve . . . . . . warm with ice cream or whipped topping.
Yields . . . . . . 12 servings.

Minnie Bell Wren
Xi Beta, Jackson, Mississippi

CHERRY CRUNCH

1 box white cake mix
1/2 c. melted butter
2 cans cherry pie filling
1/2 c. chopped pecans

Combine . . . . cake mix and butter in bowl, mixing until crumbly.
Layer . . . . . . pie filling and cake mix in 9 x 13-inch baking pan.
Top . . . . with pecans.
Bake . . . . at 350 degrees for 25 to 30 minutes or until browned.
Yields . . . . . . 12 servings.

Patricia A. Reed
Xi Alpha Pi, Funkstown, Maryland

CHERRY-PINEAPPLE DESSERT

1   21-oz. can cherry pie filling
1   14-oz. can crushed pineapple
1 box yellow cake mix
3/4 c. chopped walnuts
3/4 c. coconut
1 c. melted margarine

Combine . . . . pie filling and pineapple in 9 x 13-inch baking pan, mixing well.
Layer . . . . . . cake mix, walnuts and coconut over fruit.
Pour . . . . margarine evenly over top.
Bake . . . . at 350 degrees for 30 to 35 minutes or until bubbly; cool.
Garnish . . . . . with whipped topping.
Yields . . . . . . 12-15 servings.

Virginia E. Johnson
Preceptor Alpha Nu, The Dalles, Oregon

DIAMOND HEAD CRUNCH

1 med. can crushed pineapple
1 can apple pie filling
1 pkg. dry lemonade mix
1 box yellow cake mix
1 stick butter
1/2 c. chopped nuts
1/2 c. coconut

Layer . . . . . . first 4 ingredients in 9 x 13-inch baking pan.
Dot . . . . with butter.
Top . . . . with nuts and coconut.
Bake . . . . at 350 degrees for 1 hour.
Yields . . . . . . 8-10 servings.

Karen McAndrew-Acker
Beta Omega, Allentown, Pennsylvania

EASY FRUIT PIE FILLING CAKE

2 cans fruit pie filling
1 box yellow cake mix
1 c. melted butter
1 c. chopped nuts

Layer . . . . . . pie filling, cake mix, butter and nuts in greased 9 x 13-inch baking pan.
Bake . . . . at 350 degrees for 50 minutes or until golden brown.
Serve . . . . . . with whipped cream or ice cream.
Yields . . . . . . 12 servings.

Lois Winslow
Preceptor Delta Upsilon, Fairfield, California

STRAWBERRY-RHUBARB DUMP CAKE

1   16-oz. package frozen strawberries, thawed
1 c. chopped frozen rhubarb
1 pkg. white cake mix
1 stick butter

Layer . . . . . . strawberries, rhubarb and cake mix in buttered 9 x 13-inch baking dish.
Dot . . . . with butter.
Bake . . . . at 350 degrees for 40 minutes or until cake tests done.
Yields . . . . . . 12 servings.

Janice Wilson
Lambda Mu, Gower, Missouri

Microwave
& Crock·Pot

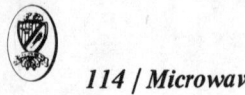

Microwave

CHILI POT ROAST

1 2 to 2 1/2-lb. chuck roast,
   1 3/4 in. thick, trimmed
1 med. onion, cut into rings
1 med. green pepper, thinly sliced
1 can tomato soup
1/2 soup can beer
2 tsp. instant beef bouillon
1 tsp. each oregano, chili powder
1 15-oz. can chili beans, drained
1 7-oz. can niblet corn, drained

Slash . . . . fat edges of chuck roast; pierce both sides with fork.
Cut . . . . into 4 pieces.
Place . . . . in glass casserole.
Top . . . . with onion and green pepper.
Combine . . . . next 5 ingredients in bowl, mixing well.
Pour . . . . over beef.
Microwave . . covered, on High for 10 minutes.
Microwave . . on Low for 30 minutes; turn beef over.
Spoon . . . . . . beans and corn over top.
Microwave . . covered, on Low for 30 minutes or until beef is tender.
Let . . . . stand, covered, for 20 minutes.

Mary Nita Wing
Laureate Alpha Eta, Lake Jackson, Texas

MICROWAVE MEAT LOAF

1 c. bread crumbs
1/2 c. milk
2 lb. ground round
2 tomatoes, chopped
1/4 c. each chopped onion, green pepper

Combine . . . . bread crumbs and milk in large bowl.
Add . . . . remaining 4 ingredients, mixing well.
Shape . . . . . . into loaf in 8 x 10-inch glass baking dish.
Microwave . . loosely covered, on Medium for 12 to 15 minutes or until cooked through.
Yields . . . . . . 6-8 servings.

Verba Allen
Xi Delta Upsilon, Miami, Oklahoma

CHOW MEIN HOT DISH

1 lb. ground beef, crumbled
1 c. each chopped onion, celery
1/2 c. chopped green pepper
1 c. minute rice
1 can each cream of mushroom, chicken with rice soup
1/4 c. soy sauce
2 tbsp. Worcestershire sauce
Chow mein noodles

Brown . . . . . . ground beef with onion, celery and green pepper in 3-quart glass casserole on High for 5 minutes; drain.
Add . . . . next 5 ingredients and 1 cup water, mixing well.
Microwave . . on High for 18 to 20 minutes, stirring occasionally.
Top . . . . with chow mein noodles.
Yields . . . . . . 6 servings.

Judy L. Roddel
Alpha Omicron, Sioux Falls, South Dakota

MEXICAN LAYER CASSEROLE

1 lb. ground beef, crumbled
1 med. onion, chopped
1 16-oz. can refried beans
1 pkg. dry enchilada sauce mix
1 8-oz. can tomato sauce
1 c. crumbled tortilla chips
1 c. shredded Cheddar cheese
1/4 c. sliced ripe olives
2 c. shredded lettuce
1 med. tomato, chopped
Sour cream (opt.)

Microwave . . ground beef with onion in 2-quart glass casserole on High for 5 to 6 minutes or until brown, stirring once; drain.
Stir . . . . in beans, enchilada sauce mix, tomato sauce and 1/2 cup water.
Microwave . . for 6 to 7 minutes longer or until bubbly, stirring once.
Layer . . . . . . chips, ground beef mixture, cheese and olives in 8 x 12-inch glass baking dish.
Microwave . . for 2 to 2 1/2 minutes or until cheese is melted.

Top . . . . with lettuce, tomato and sour cream.
Yields . . . . . . 6-8 servings.

Barbara Nagengast
Alpha Rho, Sidney, Montana

GROUND BEEF-RICE CASSEROLE

1 stalk celery, finely chopped
1/4 green pepper, finely chopped
2 cloves of garlic, minced
1/4 c. chopped green onion tops
1/4 c. chopped parsley
1 tbsp. oil
1 lb. ground beef, crumbled
3 c. cooked rice
1 can each cream of mushroom, onion soup
Salt and pepper to taste

Combine . . . . first 6 ingredients in 3-quart glass casserole.
Microwave . . on High for 4 to 5 minutes or until vegetables are tender-crisp.
Add . . . . ground beef.
Brown . . . . . . on High for 2 to 4 minutes, stirring once; drain.
Mix . . . . in rice, soups and seasonings.
Microwave . . on High for 4 to 5 minutes or to 150 degrees with temperature probe.
Yields . . . . . . 6 servings.

Betty Gaile Manlove
Preceptor Upsilon, Muncie, Indiana

SPAGHETTI PIE

1 7-oz. package spaghetti, cooked, drained
2 tbsp. butter, softened
1/3 c. Parmesan cheese
2 eggs, well beaten
1 lb. ground beef, crumbled
1/2 c. chopped onion
8 oz. canned whole tomatoes
1 6-oz. can tomato paste
1 tsp. each sugar, oregano
1/2 tsp. garlic powder
1 c. cottage cheese
1/2 c. shredded mozzarella cheese

Combine . . . . first 4 ingredients in bowl, mixing well.
Press . . . . into 10-inch glass pie plate.
Microwave . . on High for 2 minutes.
Combine . . . . ground beef and onion in glass bowl, mixing well.
Microwave . . on High for 5 minutes; drain.
Stir . . . . in tomatoes, tomato paste and seasonings.
Microwave . . covered, on High for 3 to 3 1/2 minutes or until bubbly, stirring once.
Layer . . . . . . cottage cheese and ground beef mixture into prepared pie plate.
Microwave . . loosely covered, on High for 6 to 7 minutes.
Top . . . . with mozzarella cheese.
Microwave . . for 1 minute longer or until cheese is melted.
Let . . . . stand for 10 minutes before serving.
Yields . . . . . . 6-8 servings.

Marsha Swanson
Iota Phi, West Bend, Iowa

STROGANOFF BEEFBURGER

1 can cream of mushroom soup
3 tbsp. flour
1 lb. ground chuck, crumbled
1 lg. onion, chopped
1 clove of garlic, minced
1 7-oz. can mushroom stems and pieces
1 tsp. salt
1/4 tsp. pepper
1/4 c. shredded sharp Cheddar cheese (opt.)
1 2-oz. jar chopped pimento (opt.)
1 c. sour cream
2 tbsp. chopped parsley

Blend . . . . . . soup and flour in bowl.
Add . . . . next 8 ingredients, mixing well.
Place . . . . in 3-quart glass baking dish.
Microwave . . covered, for 15 to 18 minutes.
Stir . . . . in sour cream.
Sprinkle . . . . with parsley.
Serve . . . . over rice.
Yields . . . . . . 6 servings.

Velma Emig
Preceptor Delta Alpha, Bucyrus, Ohio

EASY LASAGNA

1 lb. ground beef, crumbled
1 med. jar spaghetti sauce
Salt and pepper to taste
1 tsp. each garlic salt, oregano
1 8-oz. package lasagna noodles
16 oz. ricotta cheese
16 oz. mozzarella cheese, shredded
Chopped parsley
Parmesan cheese

Cook . . . . ground beef in glass baking dish on High until brown.
Mix . . . . in next 5 ingredients.
Spread . . . . . a small amount of sauce over bottom of 9 x 13-inch glass baking dish.
Layer . . . . . . half the uncooked noodles, ricotta cheese, mozzarella cheese, all the parsley and half the remaining sauce in baking dish.
Repeat . . . . . layers with remaining ingredients, ending with sauce.
Sprinkle . . . . with Parmesan cheese.
Microwave . . loosely covered, on High for 25 to 30 minutes, turning once.
Let . . . . stand for 5 minutes before cutting.
Yields . . . . . . 8 servings.

Christina Maribona
Xi Eta Tau, Key West, Florida

LOVELAND MICRO BURGER

1 lb. lean ground beef, crumbled
1 1/2 c. noodles
1/2 med. onion, chopped
1 16-oz. can peas, partially drained
1 1/2 c. tomato juice
1/2 tsp. salt
1/4 tsp. pepper

Layer . . . . . . ground beef, noodles, onion and peas in 2-quart glass casserole.
Pour . . . . tomato juice over all.
Microwave . . covered, on High for 15 minutes.
Stir . . . . in salt and pepper.
Microwave . . uncovered, for 3 minutes longer.
Yields . . . . . . 4-6 servings.

E. Jean Kosch
Preceptor Beta Nu, Loveland, Colorado

BAKED CHICKEN SALAD

3 c. chopped cooked chicken
2 c. sliced celery
3 to 4 oz. slivered almonds
1 2-oz. jar sliced pimento, drained
3 tbsp. lemon juice
1 tbsp. grated onion
Salt and pepper to taste
1 c. mayonnaise
1 c. crushed potato chips
1 c. shredded cheese

Combine . . . . all ingredients except potato chips and cheese in bowl, mixing well.
Spoon . . . . . . into 9 x 13-inch glass casserole.
Layer . . . . . . potato chips and cheese over top.
Microwave . . on Medium for 10 minutes.
Yields . . . . . . 6-8 servings.

Jean L. Kuhn
Xi Iota, Wyoming, Michigan

CHICKEN CORDON BLEU

2 chicken breasts, skinned, boned
4 1-oz. slices Swiss cheese
4 1-oz. slices ham
4 tbsp. flour
1 egg, beaten
1/2 c. fine dry bread crumbs
2 tbsp. butter

Pound . . . . . . chicken to flatten.
Cut . . . . into 4 pieces.
Place . . . . 1 slice cheese and 1 slice ham on each piece, folding in ends and rolling to enclose filling; secure with toothpicks.
Dust . . . . . . with flour.
Dip . . . . in egg.
Coat . . . . . . with bread crumbs.
Place . . . . in glass baking dish.
Dot . . . . with butter and season to taste.
Microwave . . loosely covered, on High for 4 minutes.
Microwave . . uncovered, for 2 minutes longer or until chicken is cooked through.
Yields . . . . . . 4 servings.

Ginger E. Harrington
Alpha Phi, Watertown, South Dakota
Beverly J. Duncan
Sigma Sigma, Jefferson, Missouri

EASY MICROWAVE CHICKEN

1/3 c. corn flake crumbs
1/4 tsp. salt
1/8 tsp. curry powder
Dash of paprika
1 chicken breast, split
1/4 c. evaporated milk

Mix .... first 4 ingredients in shallow bowl.
Dip .... chicken in evaporated milk.
Coat ...... with corn flake mixture.
Place ...... in 8 x 8-inch glass baking dish.
Microwave .. loosely covered, on High for 8 minutes or until chicken is cooked through.
Yields ...... 1-2 servings.

Pauline C. Hensley
Preceptor Pi, Harlan, Kentucky

WILD RICE-TURKEY CASSEROLE

1   6-oz. package long grain and wild rice mix, cooked
1 can cream of mushroom soup
3 c. cubed cooked turkey
1 c. chopped celery
1/4 c. chopped onion
1   5-oz. can water chestnuts, drained, sliced
3 tbsp. soy sauce
1 1/2 c. buttered crumbs

Combine .... rice and soup in 3-quart glass casserole, mixing well.
Add .... next 5 ingredients and 1 cup water, mixing well.
Sprinkle .... buttered crumbs over top.
Microwave .. for 7 minutes; turn.
Microwave .. for 7 minutes longer.
Yields ...... 8 servings.

Margaret E. Lindsey
Preceptor Beta Delta, Overland Park, Kansas

SEAFOOD NEWBURG

2 tbsp. flour
2 tbsp. melted butter
1 1/2 c. cream
2 tbsp. dry wine

1 c. fresh mushrooms
1/2 tsp. salt
Dash each of onion salt, pepper
2 egg yolks, beaten
1 c. each chopped cooked lobster, shrimp
4 or 5 pastry shells

Blend ...... flour and butter in 2-quart casserole until smooth.
Add .... next 6 ingredients, mixing well.
Microwave .. on High for 5 to 6 minutes or until thick, stirring frequently.
Mix .... a small amount of hot mixture into egg yolks; stir egg yolks into hot mixture.
Microwave .. on Medium for 2 minutes, stirring frequently.
Stir .... in lobster and shrimp.
Microwave .. on High for 1 minute.
Serve .... in pastry shells.
Yields ...... 4-5 servings.

Sally Stanford
Xi Eta Pi, Ft. Lauderdale, Florida

FAVORITE TASTY TUNA CASSEROLE

1 c. elbow macaroni
3/4 c. frozen green peas
1 can cream of celery soup
1 can French-fried onion rings
Pepper to taste
1/3 c. creamy Italian salad dressing
1   6 1/2-oz. can tuna, drained
3/4 c. shredded Cheddar cheese

Cook .... macaroni and peas in 4 to 5 cups water in saucepan until macaroni is just tender; drain.
Combine .... soup, onion rings, pepper and dressing in large bowl, mixing well.
Add .... macaroni mixture and tuna, mixing lightly.
Spoon ...... into 3-quart glass casserole.
Top .... with cheese.
Microwave .. on Medium-High for 7 to 10 minutes.
Yields ...... 5 servings.

Kim J. Payne
Kappa Pi, Stillwater, Oklahoma

JERRI'S VEG-ALL CASSEROLE

1 c. chopped celery
1 tbsp. chopped onion
1 can Veg-All
1 c. shredded cheese
1/2 c. salad dressing
1 c. cracker crumbs
1 stick margarine, melted

Combine .... first 5 ingredients in buttered glass casserole.
Top .... with cracker crumbs.
Drizzle ..... margarine over top.
Microwave .. on High for 10 minutes.
Yields ...... 12 servings.

Launa Purvis
Preceptor Beta Upsilon, Stephenville, Texas

MICROWAVE SPRING VEGETABLE MEDLEY

2 tbsp. butter, melted
1/2 lb. fresh asparagus spears, cut
*   into 2-in. pieces*
1/2 tsp. basil
1/8 tsp. pepper
1/2 lb. fresh mushrooms, sliced
1 med. tomato, cut into wedges
1/2 tsp. salt

Combine .... first 4 ingredients in 1 1/2-quart glass baking dish, mixing well.
Microwave .. covered, on High for 3 minutes.
Add .... mushrooms, mixing well.
Microwave .. covered, for 3 minutes.
Stir .... in tomato.
Microwave .. covered, for 1 1/2 minutes.
Mix .... in salt.
Let .... stand, covered, for 3 minutes before serving.
Yields ...... 4 servings.

Photograph for this recipe on page 113.

CREAMY MACARONI AND CHEESE

5 tbsp. flour
1/4 c. butter, melted
1 tsp. salt
2 c. milk

2 c. grated sharp Cheddar cheese
1 7-oz. package elbow macaroni, cooked

Blend ...... flour, butter and salt in 1-quart glass bowl.
Stir .... in milk until smooth.
Microwave .. on High for 5 to 6 minutes or until thick, stirring every minute.
Add .... cheese, stirring until melted.
Combine .... with macaroni in large glass baking dish, mixing well.
Microwave .. on Medium-High for 7 to 10 minutes or until heated through, stirring twice.
Yields ...... 6 servings.

Jo Ann Smith
Preceptor Theta Upsilon, Fortuna, California

ORANGE BREAKFAST RING

Graham cracker crumbs
1/2 c. finely chopped pecans
1/4 c. sugar
1/2 c. orange juice
1 egg
2 c. buttermilk biscuit mix
1/2 c. orange marmalade
1 orange half
1 c. butter, softened
1 tsp. grated orange rind

Coat .... greased 10-cup glass tube pan with graham cracker crumbs and pecans.
Mix .... sugar, juice, egg and biscuit mix in bowl.
Blend ...... in marmalade.
Pour .... into prepared pan.
Microwave .. on Medium for 5 minutes, turning once.
Microwave .. on High for 1 to 5 minutes or until cooked through.
Let .... stand for 5 minutes.
Invert ...... onto serving plate.
Remove .... pulp from orange, reserving shell.
Mix .... butter and orange rind in bowl.
Spoon ...... into orange shell.
Place .... in center of cake.
Yields ...... 10 servings.

Mrs. Tenny Collins
Xi Gamma, Cheyenne, Wyoming

Crock•Pot

SLO-COOK BARBECUED BEEF

1 1 1/2-lb. chuck steak, cut into
   2-in. strips
2 tbsp. oil
1/2 onion, minced
1 clove of garlic, minced
2 tbsp. molasses
1/2 tsp. chili powder
3 or 4 drops of hot pepper sauce
1/3 c. catsup
1 tsp. each seasoned salt, cornstarch
1 tbsp. each vinegar, Worcestershire
   sauce
1/2 tsp. dry mustard

Brown . . . . . . steak in oil in skillet.
Place . . . . in slow cooker.
Combine . . . . remaining ingredients in bowl,
   mixing well.
Pour . . . . over steak.
Cook . . . . on Low for 5 to 6 hours, stirring
   once.
Serve . . . . on buns.
Yields . . . . . . 4-6 servings.

Carrel J. Dutt
Preceptor Beta Kappa, Hays, Kansas

COLA SHORT RIBS

2 lb. short ribs, cut into pieces
2 tbsp. flour
2 tbsp. oil
1 c. Coca-Cola
1/4 c. each mustard, catsup
1 tsp. soya sauce
1 clove of garlic, minced
1 tsp. Italian seasoning
Salt and pepper to taste

Coat . . . . short ribs with flour.
Brown . . . . . . in oil in skillet.
Place . . . . in Crock•Pot.
Mix . . . . remaining ingredients in bowl.
Pour . . . . over short ribs.
Cook . . . . on Low for 10 to 12 hours or on
   High for 5 to 6 hours.
Yields . . . . . . 6 servings.

Marion Dewar
Xi Alpha Rho, Kitchener, Ontario, Canada

BEEF CREOLE CROCK•POT

1 1/2 lb. round steak, cut into
   2-in. strips
1 c. seasoned tomato juice
1 c. finely chopped celery
1 green pepper, finely chopped
1 8-oz. can sliced mushrooms
1 pkg. frozen okra

Combine . . . . first 4 ingredients in Crock•Pot.
Cook . . . . on High for 1 hour.
Cook . . . . on Low for 7 hours.
Add . . . . mushrooms and okra, mixing
   well.
Cook . . . . on Low for 1 hour longer.
Serve . . . . over noodles.
Yields . . . . . . 8 servings.

Ruth E. Brace
Preceptor Alpha Epsilon, Longview, Washington

QUICK BEEF STROGANOFF

2 lb. stew beef, cut into 1-in. pieces
1 can French onion soup
1 can each cream of mushroom, cream
   of celery soup

Place . . . . beef, soups and 1 soup can water
   in Crock•Pot, mixing well.
Cook . . . . on Low for 8 hours, adding
   water if necessary.
Serve . . . . with noodles.
Yields . . . . . . 4-6 servings.

Elaine Laikind
Preceptor Beta Iota, Ortonville, Michigan

BEEF STEW

1 lb. stew beef, cubed
1 c. tomato juice
1 c. chopped celery
4 lg. carrots, sliced
4 potatoes, cubed
3 onions, chopped
2 tsp. salt
1 tbsp. each sugar, tapioca

Combine . . . . all ingredients in Crock•Pot.
Cook . . . . on Low for 8 hours.
Yields . . . . . . 6 servings.

Christena Faulkner
Laureate Xi, Coldwater, Michigan

JUDY'S WORKING GIRL'S STEW

2 to 3 lb. stew beef, cubed
1 env. dry onion soup mix
2 to 3 lb. frozen stew vegetables
2 to 4 lb. frozen soup vegetables
1 46-oz. can tomato juice cocktail

Place . . . . beef in Pam-sprayed Crock•Pot.
Sprinkle . . . . with soup mix.
Place . . . . vegetables on top.
Pour . . . . juice over all.
Cook . . . . on Low for 7 to 10 hours, stir-
                 ring once.
Yields . . . . . . 6 servings.

Judy Schies
Xi Kappa Tau, Dallas, Texas

HEARTY CROCK•POT DINNER

1/2 to 1 lb. ground beef (opt.)
12 oz. bacon, cut into 1-in. pieces
1 c. chopped onion
2 29-oz. cans pork and beans
1 16-oz. can each kidney beans,
*   lima beans, drained*
1 c. catsup
1/4 c. packed brown sugar
1 tbsp. liquid smoke
3 tbsp. white vinegar
1 tsp. salt
Dash of pepper

Brown . . . . . . ground beef in skillet, stirring
                 until crumbly; drain.
Cook . . . . bacon with onion in skillet until
                 onion is tender; drain.
Combine . . . . ground beef, bacon mixture and
                 r e m a i n i n g ingredients in
                 Crock•Pot, mixing well.
Cook . . . . on Low for 4 to 9 hours.
Yields . . . . . . 8-10 servings.

Shirley Marrs
Xi Gamma Rho, Lyons, Kansas

NEW ENGLAND CLAM CHOWDER

3 cans cream of potato soup
2 cans New England clam chowder
1/4 c. margarine, melted
1 sm. onion, minced
4 c. half and half
1 or 2 cans minced clams

Combine . . . . all ingredients except clams in
                 Crock•Pot, mixing well.
Cook . . . . on High for 1 3/4 hours.
Stir . . . . in clams.
Cook . . . . for 15 minutes longer.
Yields . . . . . . 10-15 servings.

Lucy Brushaber
Xi Zeta Zeta, St. Petersburg, Florida

WEISER RIVER PHEASANT

2 pheasant, cut up
2 tbsp. oil
1 can each cream of celery, cream of
*   chicken soup*
1/4 c. red wine

Brown . . . . . . pheasant in oil in skillet; remove
                 to Crock•Pot.
Add . . . . 1/2 cup water and remaining
                 ingredients.
Cook . . . . on Medium for 5 hours.
Serve . . . . over steamed rice.
Yields . . . . . . 4 servings.

Mary Thompson
Preceptor Tau, Weiser, Idaho

CHIGETTI

1 med. onion, finely chopped
1/4 c. chopped green pepper
2 cans cream of mushroom soup
1 c. chicken broth
1 8-oz. package grated cheese
1 sm. jar pimento, chopped
1 tsp. salt
1/4 tsp. pepper
4 c. chopped cooked chicken
2 1/2 c. cooked vermicelli

Saute . . . . . . onion and green pepper in
                 skillet.
Combine . . . . next 3 ingredients in large bowl,
                 mixing well.
Add . . . . sauteed vegetables, pimento,
                 salt, pepper and chicken, mixing
                 well.
Combine . . . . with vermicelli in Crock•Pot,
                 tossing lightly.
Cook . . . . on Low for 2 hours.

Lois Brewer
Eta Nu, Belton, Missouri

SLOW COOKER COQ AU VIN WITH NOODLES

1   3-lb. broiler, cut up
2 tbsp. oil
1 c. dry red wine
1/8 tsp. pepper
1 bay leaf
1/4 tsp. each thyme, garlic powder
1 sm. green pepper, diced
1/2 lb. mushrooms
Salt
3 tbsp. flour
1   16-oz. jar whole onions, drained
8 oz. medium egg noodles, cooked

Brown . . . . . . chicken in oil in skillet; pour off excess drippings.
Combine . . . . with next 7 ingredients and 1 1/4 teaspoons salt in slow cooker.
Cook . . . . covered, on Low for 4 1/2 hours.
Blend . . . . . . flour with 4 tablespoons water in bowl.
Stir . . . . into chicken mixture with onions.
Cook . . . . for 1/2 hour longer.
Serve . . . . with noodles.
Yields . . . . . . 4 servings.

Photograph for this recipe above.

FANTASTIC CHICKEN CROCK•POT DISH

1 pkg. dried beef, cut up
6 to 8 chicken breasts, boned
6 to 8 slices bacon

1/2 c. sour cream
1/2 c. flour
1 can cream of chicken soup

Arrange . . . . . dried beef on bottom of greased Crock•Pot.
Wrap . . . . each chicken breast with bacon.
Place . . . . over dried beef.
Mix . . . . sour cream and flour in bowl.
Add . . . . soup, mixing well.
Pour . . . . over chicken.
Cook . . . . on Low for 8 to 10 hours or on High for 3 to 5 hours.
Serve . . . . over rice.
Yields . . . . . . 6-8 servings.

Nancy Michael
Xi Alpha Phi, West Columbia, South Carolina

LOW-CHOLESTEROL CHICKEN

1   3 to 4-lb. chicken, cut up, skinned
1 sm. jar spaghetti sauce with mushrooms
Salt and pepper to taste

Place . . . . chicken in Crock•Pot.
Cover . . . . . . with spaghetti sauce.
Season . . . . . with salt and pepper.
Cook . . . . on High for 5 to 6 hours.
Serve . . . . over spaghetti.
Yields . . . . . . 6 servings.

Katherine Morton
Xi Upsilon Delta, Borrego Springs, California

CROCK•POT POTATOES AND HAM

6   1/4-in. thick slices ham
7 med. potatoes, peeled, thinly sliced
1 c. chopped onion
Salt and pepper to taste
1 c. grated Cheddar cheese
1 can cream of mushroom soup
Paprika

Layer . . . . . . half the ham, potatoes, onion, salt and pepper and cheese in Crock•Pot.
Repeat . . . . . layers.
Spread . . . . . soup over top, sealing to edges.
Sprinkle . . . . with paprika.
Cook . . . . on Low for 8 hours or on High for 4 hours.
Yields . . . . . . 6 servings.

Susan Jacoby
Xi Alpha Xi, Gering, Nebraska

Equivalent Chart

	WHEN RECIPE CALLS FOR:	YOU NEED:
BREAD & CEREAL	1 c. soft bread crumbs	2 slices
	1 c. fine dry bread crumbs	4-5 slices
	1 c. small bread cubes	2 slices
	1 c. fine cracker crumbs	24 saltines
	1 c. fine graham cracker crumbs	14 crackers
	1 c. vanilla wafer crumbs	22 wafers
	1 c. crushed corn flakes	3 c. uncrushed
	4 c. cooked macaroni	1 8-oz. package
	3 1/2 c. cooked rice	1 c. uncooked
DAIRY	1 c. freshly grated cheese	1/4 lb.
	1 c. cottage cheese or sour cream	1 8-oz. carton
	2/3 c. evaporated milk	1 sm. can
	1 2/3 c. evaporated milk	1 tall can
	1 c. whipped cream	1/2 c. heavy cream
SWEET	1 c. semisweet chocolate pieces	1 6-oz. package
	2 c. granulated sugar	1 lb.
	4 c. sifted confectioners' sugar	1 lb.
	2 1/4 c. packed brown sugar	1 lb.
MEAT	3 c. diced cooked meat	1 lb., cooked
	2 c. ground cooked meat	1 lb., cooked
	4 c. diced cooked chicken	1 5-lb. chicken
NUTS	1 c. chopped nuts	4 oz. shelled
		1 lb. unshelled
VEGETABLES	4 c. sliced or diced raw potatoes	4 medium
	2 c. cooked green beans	1/2 lb. fresh or 1 16-oz. can
	1 c. chopped onion	1 large
	4 c. shredded cabbage	1 lb.
	2 c. canned tomatoes	1 16-oz. can
	1 c. grated carrot	1 large
	2 1/2 c. lima beans or red beans	1 c. dried, cooked
	1 4-oz. can mushrooms	1/2 lb. fresh
FRUIT	4 c. sliced or chopped apples	4 medium
	2 c. pitted cherries	4 c. unpitted
	3 to 4 tbsp. lemon juice plus 1 tsp. grated peel	1 lemon
	1/3 c. orange juice plus 2 tsp. grated peel	1 orange
	1 c. mashed banana	3 medium
	4 c. cranberries	1 lb.
	3 c. shredded coconut	1/2 lb.
	4 c. sliced peaches	8 medium
	1 c. pitted dates or candied fruit	1 8-oz. package
	2 c. pitted prunes	1 12-oz. package
	3 c. raisins	1 15-oz. package

COMMON EQUIVALENTS

1 tbsp. = 3 tsp.	4 qt. = 1 gal.
2 tbsp. = 1 oz.	6 1/2 to 8-oz. can = 1 c.
4 tbsp. = 1/4 oz.	10 1/2 to 12-oz. can = 1 1/4 c.
5 tbsp. + 1 tsp. = 1/3 c.	14 to 16-oz. can (No. 300) = 1 3/4 c.
8 tbsp. = 1/2 c.	16 to 17-oz. can (No. 303) = 2 c.
12 tbsp. = 3/4 c.	1-lb. 4-oz. can or 1-pt. 2-oz. can (No. 2) = 2 1/2 c.
16 tbsp. = 1 c.	1-lb. 13-oz. can (No. 2 1/2) = 3 1/2 c.
1 c. = 8 oz. or 1/2 pt.	3-lb. 3-oz. can or 46-oz. can or 1-qt. 14-oz. can = 5 3/4 c.
4 c. = 1 qt.	6 1/2-lb. or 7-lb. 5-oz. can (No. 10) = 12 to 13 c.

Substitution Chart

	INSTEAD OF:	USE:
BAKING	1 tsp. baking powder	1/4 tsp. soda plus 1/2 tsp. cream of tartar
	1 c. sifted all-purpose flour	1 c. plus 2 tbsp. sifted cake flour
	1 c. sifted cake flour	1 c. minus 2 tbsp. sifted all-purpose flour
	1 tsp. cornstarch (for thickening)	2 tbsp. flour or 1 tbsp. tapioca
SWEET	1 1-oz. square chocolate	3 to 4 tbsp. cocoa plus 1 tsp. shortening
	1 2/3 oz. semisweet chocolate	1 oz. unsweetened chocolate plus 4 tsp. sugar
	1 c. granulated sugar	1 c. packed brown sugar or 1 c. corn syrup, molasses, honey minus 1/4 c. liquid
	1 c. honey	1 to 1 1/4 c. sugar plus 1/4 c. liquid or 1 c. molasses or corn syrup
DAIRY	1 c. sweet milk	1 c. sour milk or buttermilk plus 1/2 tsp. soda
	1 c. sour milk	1 c. sweet milk plus 1 tbsp. vinegar or lemon juice of 1 c. buttermilk
	1 c. buttermilk	1 c. sour milk or 1 c. yogurt
	1 c. light cream	7/8 c. skim milk plus 3 tbsp. butter
	1 c. heavy cream	3/4 c. skim milk plus 1/3 c. butter
	1 c. sour cream	7/8 c. sour milk plus 3 tbsp. butter
	1 c. bread crumbs	3/4 c. cracker crumbs
SEASONINGS	1 c. catsup	1 c. tomato sauce plus 1/2 c. sugar plus 2 tbsp. vinegar
	1 tbsp. prepared mustard	1 tsp. dry mustard
	1 tsp. Italian spice	1/4 tsp. each oregano, basil, thyme, rosemary plus dash of cayenne
	1 tsp. allspice	1/2 tsp. cinnamon plus 1/8 tsp. cloves
	1 medium onion	1 tbsp. dried minced onion or 1 tsp. onion powder
	1 clove of garlic	1/8 tsp. garlic powder or 1/8 tsp. instant minced garlic or 3/4 tsp. garlic salt or 5 drops of liquid garlic
	1 tsp. lemon juice	1/2 tsp. vinegar

Index

Library of Congress Cataloging in Publication Data
Main entry under title:
All-occasion casseroles cookbook with menus.
  Includes index.
  1. Casserole cookery. 2. Menus. I. Beta Sigma Phi.
TX693.A437 1983 641.18'21 83-14045
ISBN 0-87197-156-9

FAVORITE RECIPES OF®
BETA SIGMA PHI INTERNATIONAL

COOKBOOKS

Add to
Your Cookbook Collection
Select from These ALL-TIME
Favorites

BOOK TITLE	ITEM NUMBER
Holiday (1971) 288 Pages	70041
The Golden Anniversary Cookbook (1980) 200 Pages	11665
Desserts & Party Foods Cookbook (1982) 128 Pages	20370
All-Occasion Casseroles Cookbook with Menus (1983) 128 Pages	28037

FOR ORDERING INFORMATION

Write to:
Favorite Recipes Press
P. O. Box 77
Nashville, Tennessee 37202

BOOKS OFFERED SUBJECT TO AVAILABILITY.